THE PLAIN ENGLISH APPROACH TO
BUSINESS WRITING

The Plain English Approach to Business Writing

REVISED EDITION

EDWARD P. BAILEY, JR.

OXFORD UNIVERSITY PRESS
New York   Oxford

Oxford University Press

Oxford   New York
Athens   Auckland   Bangkok   Bogotá   Bombay
Buenos Aires   Calcutta   Cape Town   Dar es Salaam
Delhi   Florence   Hong Kong   Istanbul   Karachi
Kuala Lumpur   Madras   Madrid   Melbourne
Mexico City   Nairobi   Paris   Singapore
Taipei   Tokyo   Toronto

and associated companies in
Berlin   Ibadan

Published by Oxford University Press, Inc.
198 Madison Avenue, New York, New York 10016

Oxford is a registered trademark of Oxford University Press

Library of Congress Cataloging-in-Publication Data
Bailey, Edward P.
The plain English approach to business writing/
Edward P. Bailey, Jr.
Includes index.
ISBN 0-19-511565-1 (pbk.)
1. Business writing.   I. Title.
HF5718.3.B35   1997   808'.06665—dc21   96-45541

1 3 5 7 9 8 6 4 2

Printed in the United States of America

For my wife, Janet,

and daughters, Laura and Jeannette

Acknowledgments

I continue to express my gratitude to two people who helped lead me to plain English many years ago. One I never met: Rudolf Flesch. But I read his books and found them wonderfully motivating. The other person, Dr. Tom Murawski, is one of my best friends. He gave me one of those books by Flesch and has inspired me ever since.

Other people have been very helpful:

- Janet Hiller, my wife, who read and commented on everything. She is terrific.

- Brooke Bailey (my brother) and Cathy Bailey (his wife) for their excellent advice on the draft of this book.

- Sister P. J. Cahill and Professors Joan Feeney, Charles Hurst, Arthur Meiners, Robert Sigethy, and Maribeth Wyvill—my colleagues at Marymount University.

- Drs. Jim Gaston, Terry Bangs, and Bill Wallisch—friends, colleagues, and professional inspiration for nearly 20 years.

- Don Insko, who made important contributions to the graphical elements of this book.

- Dr. Fred Kiley, Dr. Greg Foster, Dr. Joe Goldberg, and Ms. Judy Clark—my friends at the National Defense University.

- Marilou and Edward Bailey, my parents; Jeannette and Laura, my daughters; and Jeannette's husband, Max Boot. They provided inspiration.

My thanks to my students—both at Marymount University and in classes I have taught to my business clients—who contributed excellent examples of plain English for this book

Finally, my appreciation to Susan Chang and Linda Robbins at Oxford University Press: I am indeed fortunate to have worked with Oxford and with them.

Fairfax Station, Virginia   E. P. B.
October 1996

Contents

THE NEW WAY
TO WRITE

CHAPTER 1

What is plain English?

Bottom line

Plain English is easier to read—and easier to write. It can express the range of ideas, from simple to complex.

When I first came across plain English, I was teaching writing in college. You can guess what I had been teaching: an overly formal style designed more to impress than simply to communicate clearly to the reader.

Since then, I've switched to plain English and taught it extensively—in college and to many thousands of people in government and business. This book is a result of those experiences, and it's designed to help you discover plain English.

When you make that discovery, you will find that writing is much easier for you—and it will be better, too.

What is plain English?

Plain English, to put it simply, is a way of expressing your ideas clearly. Throughout the book, I talk of plain English as having three parts:

- *Style*. By style, I mean how to write clear, readable sentences. My advice is simple: write more the way you talk. This may sound simple, but it's a powerful metaphor that can revolutionize your writing.

- *Organization.* I suggest starting with your main point almost all the time. That doesn't mean it has to be your first sentence (though it can be)—just that it should come early and be extremely easy to find.

- *Layout.* This is the appearance of the page and your words on it. Headings, bullets, and other techniques of white space help your reader see—visually—the underlying structure of your writing. The value is immense. I think of layout as fun to do, and easy, too, with today's computers.

Plain English is not limited to expressing only simple ideas: it works for all kinds of writing—from an internal memo to a complicated technical report. It can handle any level of complexity.

What *isn't* plain English?

Businessese isn't plain English, nor is academese, bureau-cratese, legalese, or any other "-ese."

Here's an example of some businessese from a federal regulation:

> Each application shall be supported by a comprehensive letter of explanation in duplicate. This letter shall set forth all the facts required to present to this office a complete disclosure of the transaction.

Those of you with business experience know this example is just beginning businessese, relatively uncomplicated compared with what the true Masters of Gobbledygook can turn out.

Nevertheless, it could be more straightforward. Here's a better version. Notice that it loses no preciseness:

You must send us the following:

- one copy of your application
- two copies of a letter explaining the complete details of your transaction

See the difference? You can understand the first version with a little effort, but you'd hate to read several paragraphs—or pages—in that style. The second version won't win the Nobel Prize for literature, but it *is* straightforward communication.

And, at times, plain English does approach art. A clean, straightforward document can be beautiful in its simplicity and efficiency.

Why is plain English better than the "other way"?

Plain English has two important advantages over the other way of writing:

- It's far easier for your reader to read.
- It's far easier for you to write.

You don't need many more advantages than those, do you? But let's look further.

In the past, plain English seemed merely a preference: you like the old way; I like plain English. Who's to decide? Well, psycholinguists have simplified the decision. Their work shows clearly that plain English is easier for all of us to read, no matter how smart we are. And no matter how much experience we have as readers.

For example, psycholinguists have learned that we all take longer to read less familiar words (like *commence*) than familiar ones (like *begin*). The difference is only a few hundred milliseconds in time—but a lot less strain on the short-term memory (and the older I get, the less strain I want to put on mine).

The implication? As writers, we can help our readers by preferring ordinary words.

That's just one very brief example of what the psycholinguists have been up to. I investigate their work at length in another book, *Writing Clearly: A Contemporary Approach*.

Because of the work of psycholinguists, writing style is no longer like the width of lapels: "What's the style this year—wide or narrow?" Instead, there's solid scientific underpinning for the plain English movement.

There's a further reason for writing plain English, too.

Suppose you're the boss—a manager with 15 people working for you. A prestigious project comes in, requiring a report. Only two of your people are both qualified to work on it and have time available:

- One has a straightforward style that's easy for you and your client to understand.

- The other laboriously churns out complex, bureaucratic products that make you reach for the aspirin bottle.

Who will you choose?

If you assign the project to the bad writer, you know you'll have to do extensive rewriting (and maybe most of the writing, too). On the other hand, if you assign the project to the good writer, you can do what you're paid to do: manage. And the final product will be much better because you can spend your time evaluating drafts for content instead of struggling simply to decipher them.

Who is writing plain English these days?

It's hard to believe, but many people still write businessese. But many have also shifted to plain English. In other words, there's a "fence"—with some people on the bureaucratic side and others on the plain English side.

Fortunately, more and more people are moving to the plain English side—and when people reach that side, they never jump back. The advantages of plain English are just too obvious.

Also, many large organizations today are endorsing plain English:

- *Private business.* Many successful companies require plain English. Major improvement in writing has occurred in the fields of insurance, computers, banking, and health care.

- *Federal agencies.* Many (perhaps *most*) federal agencies are training their people to write in plain English.

- *U.S. military.* Each military service strongly urges plain English—by regulation (and those regulations are in plain English, too).

- *Scientific and engineering organizations.* Many of these organizations have to be able to express their ideas to lay people.

- *And even lawyers!* Too many lawyers still depend on the language of the Magna Charta, but even this "iceberg" is starting to slide into the sea. There are, for example, sample wills and other standard documents available to lawyers in plain English.

The move today is clearly toward plain English because it works. It can work for you, too. This book will show you how to write it.

What's the book's structure?

The next three chapters introduce the three fundamentals of writing in plain English: style, organization, and layout. The rest of this part of the book then goes into more detail on each of the fundamentals.

For example, after you get the fundamentals of layout in Chapter 4, later chapters will cover other topics of layout such as choosing typefaces, designing effective headings, and using graphics. There are chapters expanding on style and organization, too.

❖   ❖   ❖

So let's begin the journey. For many, it has changed their lives. I know it has changed mine.

CHAPTER 2

Style: writing a
readable sentence

Bottom line

*Write more the way you talk—with ordinary words, a variety of
punctuation, personal pronouns, and contractions.*

Let's start with a quiz. Choose "a" or "b":

> How have you produced most of the words in your life?
> a. by writing them
> b. by speaking them

For most of us, the answer is "b": we've *spoken* many more
words than we've written.

"What does that have to do with writing?" you may ask.

Everything. You see, in plain English, words and sentences
are more like those in spoken English. Spoken English is
the language we're most comfortable with—the language
that works for us.

That's why most professional writers use spoken English
when they write. Check the editorial section of your newspaper. What do you find there?

If your paper is typical, you'll find the editors use spoken
English. Look in one of the most popular papers in the
world: the *Wall Street Journal.* You'll certainly find spoken
English there.

In fact, the biggest headline on page one of every *Wall Street Journal* is "What's News—." The contraction makes the tone informal, and the dash leads the reader into the text that follows. Informal tone and awareness of the reader are two common characteristics of plain English.

The key advice: "Write the way you talk"

Thus, the key to plain English is this: talk to your reader. Simply talk on paper. Write the way you talk.

Imagine you're actually standing in front of your reader. Or talking on the telephone. What would you say—in an organized and polite way? Then write those words.

Sound simplistic? Some people are afraid that "writing the way you talk" means being simple-minded, writing like a kindergartner. But that would be true only if you talk like a kindergartner. The advice is to write the way *you* talk. Look for spoken English: look in magazines, newspapers, successful books. And *listen* for it, too: listen to the most moving speeches, the best newscasts.

What you will find is that the best of writing and the best of speaking have much in common. And what they have in common produces plain English.

Should we *really* write the way we talk?

Well . . . we don't want to write the way we sometimes talk, complete with the occasional "uhs" and rambling, disconnected sentences.

But if you imagine a reader in front of you, if you imagine you are actually talking on paper to that reader, the words will come out like the best of speaking—and the best of writing, too.

Tip

For the next thing you write, try putting down the words as you would actually say them. That's what I do: I sit in front of a computer, "talking" through the keyboard to my imaginary reader.

Don't worry about the theoretical differences between writing and speaking. Simply talk on paper.

Specific tips for writing the way you talk

To talk on paper, you may have to change your writing. For example, when you write:

- Do you normally use words like *commence* instead of *begin,* and *prior to* instead of *before?*

- Do you normally avoid all marks of punctuation except the period and the comma?

- Do you normally avoid using any personal pronouns— like *I, we,* and *you?*

If so, you're a typical bureaucratic writer. Get ready to take the most important step in your writing career. Here's what I suggest:

- Use ordinary words.

- Use a variety of punctuation.

- Use more personal pronouns.

- Use contractions.

If you're like me before I began writing plain English, these suggestions may seem like heresy, like crimes against the English language. Now, though, I think I committed my crimes before I followed these suggestions—not after.

Let's examine those four suggestions in more detail.

Use ordinary words

Which column do you normally choose your words from when you're writing?

advise	tell
assist	help
commence	begin
furnish	give
prior to	before

If you're the way I used to be, you probably choose from the left-hand side.

In fact, when I first saw a list like this, I was shocked to find that I chose *most* of my words from the left-hand side. And I could have given you very good reasons, too—something to do with nuances of meaning.

Then I noticed that when I spoke I consistently used words from the *right-hand* side. Why were the nuances so important when I wrote but not when I talked?

After serious soul-searching, I realized that the so-called nuances weren't really there at all. Instead, I had come to believe that I needed to write with a formal tone—that was the real reason I was choosing the more "impressive" words. As a result, I'd stopped writing with my most important vocabulary: the words I use in speaking each day.

So here's my advice on words. Do as the good professionals do:

- Good professionals use *ordinary* words unless they need something more precise—which happens fairly often.

- But bad amateurs use *impressive* words all the time—unless they can't think of them.

To see what I mean, let's look at writing by a successful professional, Russell Baker. This is the first paragraph of one of his books, *Growing Up* (which won the Pulitzer Prize). He's telling us about his mother, who's in a nursing home but doesn't realize she's there. She's living in the past.

As you read, notice that the passage says *extraordinary* things with *ordinary* words:

> At the age of eighty my mother had her last bad fall, and after that her mind wandered free through time. Some days she went to weddings and funerals that had taken place half a century earlier. On others she presided over family dinners cooked on Sunday afternoons for children who were now gray with age. Through all this, she lay in bed but moved across time, traveling among the dead decades with a speed and an ease beyond the gift of physical science.

Absolutely terrific, isn't it? And where are the "impressive" words? About the only one is *presided*—a good choice that gives us the sense of the matriarch, the woman in control. As I said, such choices help with preciseness.

But ordinary words are precise, too. Do any of Baker's phrases stand out as especially nice? I like "her mind wandered free through time." Where's the "impressive" word there? There isn't one—yet the idea is far from ordinary or simple. And preciseness? The word *wandered*—a perfectly plain word—is right on target.

Writing with ordinary words doesn't mean writing with kindergarten language or producing only simple-minded ideas.

Writing with "impressive" words does mean making the reader's job harder. Even though we know all the words in the left-hand column, we have more trouble reading them, particularly if many appear in the same sentence or paragraph. And they usually do if writers consistently choose their words from the left-hand side.

For example, let's look at a sentence with mainly impressive words:

> Subsequent to the passage of subject legislation, it is incumbent upon you to advise your organization to comply with it.

And if we rewrite that sentence with ordinary words:

> After the law passes, you must tell your people to comply with it.

Would you rather read pages of the first version or the second?

By the way, the second version keeps the phrase "comply with it." It could have said something like "follow it," but the word *comply* seems to make the message a little more urgent. So I don't suggest you always choose the ordinary word. But—to use a word from computer terminology— make ordinary words your *default*. Choose other words if preciseness demands, just as you do when you speak.

And ask yourself what words Russell Baker (the professional who wrote about his mother) would choose if he were writing your document.

For a list of simpler words and phrases, see Appendix A.

Use a variety of punctuation

The second suggestion on style is to use a variety of punctuation. Too often business writers use only periods and commas.

Have you ever heard anybody speak in a monotone? Well, people who write with only periods and commas are like speakers who speak in a monotone, forcing you—the audience—to do too much work: "What was important in that sentence? What's going to be carried over to the next sentence?" The audience has to figure that out because the speaker, using a monotone, isn't helping.

Good speakers do help, though. They use hand gestures and voice inflection to help their listeners along. Good writers, using spoken English, allow punctuation to replace those hand gestures and that voice inflection.

This chapter doesn't cover all the important marks of punctuation you need to learn. A later chapter does that. But this chapter does look at one easy punctuation mark— the question mark—to illustrate the need for more than periods and commas.

A number of years ago, someone asked if I ever used questions in my writing. I realized that I never did, and I didn't know why. So let me ask you now: "Do you use questions in your writing? If you look at the last ten pages you've written, will you find any?"

If your answer is "yes," you know one of the secrets of effective writing. If your answer is "no," that means you're generating your sentences very differently when you write and when you talk—undoubtedly, you use questions often in your talking. And the sentence structure in good talking is better than the sentence structure in typical bureaucratic writing.

So let's look more closely at when to use questions in writing. One time is when you really have a question:

- When does the new copying machine get here?

- How far is Santa Fe from Albuquerque?

Too often, though, people "write around" the question: "Request this office be informed of when the copying machine will be delivered." The shift away from the question is a shift toward writing in a monotone. Your question—often the very purpose for writing—loses emphasis, doesn't it? So don't avoid the question mark when you're asking for something. The reader will more likely take notice of the question because of the emphasis it receives.

Now let's focus on another time to use the question: the question that you, the writer, will answer. Such questions focus what you're saying and emphasize your answer—just as vocal inflection and hand gestures do when you're talking. In other words, such questions draw the reader in.

Let's look at an example. Here's some writing in a monotone (without questions):

> The main point is that the defective computer disks are not the responsibility of the manufacturer, as we first suspected, but of the wholesaler, who stored them at a 130 degree temperature.

Now let's add questions:

> Just who's responsible for the defective computer disks? Is it the manufacturer, as we first suspected? No. The *wholesaler* is responsible—he stored them at a 130 degree temperature.

See the difference questions make? I know. I cheated. In addition to the question mark, I also used a really short sentence ("No."), italics, and a dash.

You don't need to use these techniques in every line you write. But if you're not using them at all, then you're probably communicating with far less emphasis in writing than in speaking.

So the message is to use a variety of punctuation to control your emphasis and replace the hand gestures and voice inflection we all use in speaking. The question mark is one easy way to start. Chapter 8 tells you about other important marks.

Use more personal pronouns

Now for an even more important question: "Do you ever use personal pronouns in your writing?" In some audiences I speak to, about half the people say yes. In others, almost everyone uses them. In still other audiences, almost no one. Yet the value of using them is immense.

In fact, I've never worked with an organization that avoided pronouns and wrote clearly.

Here are the important pronouns for plain English:

> First person: *I, me, my, mine, we, us, our, ours*
>
> Second person: *you, your, yours*

Many of us learned at some time not to use these personal pronouns. That idea comes partly from the outdated notion that important business writing must be formal.

Yet the notion of what makes good writing is changing, and a more personal, informal tone is gaining wide acceptance for all kinds of writing.

Another reason people write without personal pronouns is to seem more objective—as though removing pronouns (especially first person) somehow removes all human fallibility. I remember asking one of the top executives in a federal agency what he felt about his people using first person pronouns.

The conversation went like this:

> Me: "Some of your people feel they shouldn't use first person—*I, me, we*—in their writing because they'd seem to be giving their opinions. What do you think?"

> Him: "I *hire* people for their opinions! Personal pronouns are an *excellent* way for them to express their opinions—to me and to anyone else."

Don't bosses often hire people for the judgment they can exercise—in other words, for their opinions?

Not too long ago, some organizations even objected to the second person pronoun, *you*. For example, can you imagine reading a book telling how to do something if the book never used the pronoun *you*? The early computer manuals did just that:

> The monitor must first be turned on and then the computer must be turned on. A menu with the . . .

The computer industry learned that manuals need to be user friendly. And user friendly means talking on paper to the users. Now you're more likely to find a computer manual saying this:

> First, turn on the monitor. Then turn on the computer. You'll then see a menu with . . .

The differences in these two short samples are few, but users of entire computer manuals certainly noted the change in approach (and so did the writers of those manuals and the sellers of computers and computer products!).

One reason for using pronouns is that you will more likely use active—instead of passive—voice. The passage from the old-style computer manual, for example, uses passive voice for both verbs.

Chapter 6 discusses passive voice in detail, but you've certainly heard of its bad reputation. Passive sentences are usually harder to read, especially if the content is complex or if several of them appear in a row. So one reason to use personal pronouns is that your sentences will more likely be in active voice and, thus, easier to read.

Another reason to use pronouns is that you can *write* more easily with them. Can you imagine talking without ever using personal pronouns? I try that experiment during my classes, giving a volunteer a topic and then asking the volunteer to tell us about it without using *I, me, you,* and so forth. The volunteer immediately becomes uncomfortable, stays silent a few seconds, and then begins with something like this: "Uh."

Without exception, the volunteers say that trying to talk without personal pronouns is extremely difficult. They also report that when they do find words to speak, those words usually express different ideas—not quite what the volunteers wanted to say in the first place but only what they could say.

In other words, not only was communication harder, but the content changed to meet the artificial requirement of not using the pronouns.

In business, how often do you want your people to alter their content to meet the same artificial requirement?

When we try to write without using personal pronouns—as many people do—we have to put a "mental editor" between our thoughts and the page (or computer screen). That mental editor tries desperately to strip out personal pronouns and restate the ideas without them. Writing with that mental editor is hard work. And, as most professional writers have discovered, it's unnecessary, too.

So the next time you write, talk on paper, and let the personal pronouns come naturally.

Must you always use pronouns to be a good writer? No. Some writing—just like some speaking—simply doesn't call for them. For example, if you're describing a disk drive (instead of telling how to use it), you probably won't need personal pronouns at all: "A disk drive has three major components: the housing mechanism, the drive head, and the . . .").

The key, then, isn't really to use personal pronouns: the key is to stop avoiding them. You don't try to *use* pronouns when you're talking, but you certainly don't try to *avoid* them, either, do you? Just use the same system for your writing.

So get rid of that tyrannical mental editor. And start "*un*avoiding" a few pronouns!

Use contractions

What about contractions? Will using words like *can't* and *we'll* really help your writing? In the past, I pushed contractions only very gently. This time, I'm going to give a stronger message: Yes!! Contractions can make a significant difference in your writing.

You're *much* more likely to write plain English if you use contractions. In fact, it's hard to use a contraction in a sentence and have anything else in the sentence be bureaucratic.

That is, if you're in the mode of using contractions, you're also in the mode of using ordinary words, pronouns, and the entire arsenal that makes up plain English.

In fact, if you're a boss, try encouraging your people to use contractions freely. You'll be surprised how much else in their writing changes for the better.

A concern people have is that the tone of their writing will be too chatty if they're using contractions. I don't think so. We read contractions in professional writing all the time without feeling that the tone is chatty.

For example, look at the *Wall Street Journal.* You'll see contractions throughout. Look at the motto of *The New York*

Times: "All the news that's fit to print." Some people say, "Newspapers. So what?" Well, in my experience, most newspaper editors try very hard to use a correct yet readable style. They're often a good source for usage. But, also, most other writing you enjoy—like books you pay money for—uses plain English, complete with contractions.

One agency I worked with, however, just couldn't bring itself to use contractions. We finally got to plain English, but we had to take the long way around.

Here's what happened: When people who weren't used to writing plain English tried writing without contractions, their writing reverted to typical legalese. They stopped talking on paper. So we had them start over, writing their *drafts* with contractions. The writing improved.

Then, after writing with contractions, the writers simply *un*contracted later (with help from computers). The result was plain English. But, I confess: the tone was rather stiff.

Tip

Try a contraction in the next thing you write. The first time, you may feel uncomfortable. But go ahead. You'll soon feel free, as though a burden has fallen from your shoulders as you begin to write.

What about the rules we learned in school?

At this point, you may be wondering if we should pay attention to anything we learned in school. That depends on the school, because many are terrific. And, of course, we need to follow certain rules or else communication will become hopelessly erratic.

There are three categories of rules to consider:

- rules we all agree with
- rules few people agree with
- rules amateurs follow and professionals don't

Let's look more closely at each of these.

Rules we all agree with

Some rules just aren't controversial. For example, we all know to start sentences with capital letters and end them with periods or other terminal marks of punctuation. We also want subjects to agree with verbs and pronouns to agree with the nouns they replace. There aren't really a lot of these rules that cause us a problem. For the most part, people in business know them and follow them.

Rules few people agree with

There's another category of rules "experts" on language try to foist on us. Jim Quinn, author of *American Tongue and Cheek,* calls these "experts" pop grammarians—people who seem to have a stone tablet from God filled with "The Commandments" on usage.

One of those pop grammarians, according to Quinn, is Edwin Newman, author of *Strictly Speaking.* In *Strictly Speaking,* Newman is appalled by the construction *convince to* (as in "The Soviet Union evidently is not able to *convince* Cairo *to* accept a rapid cease-fire.").

In all my teaching and consulting, I've never found another soul who agrees with Newman on that issue. Yet he calls it "one of the worst things" *The New York Times* does.

Don't worry about the pop grammarians. They're talking—and mainly arguing—only with each other. Virtually all linguists, the real experts on language, disagree with the pop grammarians.

Rules amateurs follow and professionals don't

Professionals *are* professionals because readers pay for what they write. (How much would you pay for the stuff in your in-box?)

Professionals follow the standard rules (such as beginning sentences with capital letters); they ignore almost all of the rules by the pop grammarians; and they ignore a few rules they learned in school.

What are the rules from school the professionals have learned to ignore? John Trimble, in his classic book *Writing with Style: Conversations on the Art of Writing*, lists "The Seven Nevers":

The Seven Nevers [from decades past]

1. Never begin a sentence with *and* or *but*.

2. Never use contractions.

3. Never refer to the reader as *you*.

4. Never use the first person pronoun *I*.

5. Never end a sentence with a preposition.

6. Never split an infinitive.

7. Never write a paragraph containing only a single sentence.

Trimble then says he's going to argue against all of them, "earnestly hoping that I may free you of their hold forever."

I agree. The Seven Nevers would be good rules only with a key revision. You guessed it—strike out the word *never:*

1. ~~Never~~ begin a sentence with *and* or *but*.

2. ~~Never~~ use contractions.

3. ~~Never~~ refer to the reader as *you*.

4. ~~Never~~ use the first person pronoun *I*.

5. ~~Never~~ end a sentence with a preposition.

6. ~~Never~~ split an infinitive.

7. ~~Never~~ write a paragraph containing only a single sentence.

That's what almost all professionals have learned to do. Again, just look at professional writing, and you'll see you've been reading spoken English—plain English—complete with split infinitives, one-sentence paragraphs, and sentences ending with prepositions. Just the way we talk.

And check your grammar handbook. You may be surprised to find that almost all handbooks agree with Trimble—and discourage those old-fashioned and destructive "Seven Nevers."

✣   ✣   ✣

So remember the most important lesson on style: write the way you talk! It's much easier—on your reader and on you.

You'll learn more about style in these chapters:

- Chapter 6, "Passive voice"
- Chapter 7, "Abstractness"
- Chapter 8, "Punctuation"

For now, though, let's turn to the second major part of plain English: organization.

CHAPTER 3

Organization: getting to the point

Bottom line

Make your main point easy to find.

My key advice on organization is simple: start with your main point. Tell your readers, right at the start:

- what you want them to do ("I recommend you buy a color printer")

- what your conclusion is ("Wages will increase next year"), or

- whatever your main purpose is for your document

Now, the main point doesn't have to be the first sentence (though it can be much of the time). I'm just saying that the main point should be up front—*before* your reasons instead of after.

Why do you want the main point first?

What happens if you're reading something ten pages long and the main point is *not* up front? I think most of us get confused and frustrated, so we skip to the end and hunt for it. Once we find it, we can usually start over and understand the document much better. With the context of the bottom line, the details up front start to make more sense to us.

So why do writers often put the main point at the end? Here are some common reasons I've heard:

- to make readers read the entire document
- to build the case so readers will more likely accept the main point
- to reenact how the writer learned something
- to delay bad news

Those reasons all sound good, don't they? The problem is, as I've already noted, most readers simply don't put up with that order. We'll stop reading, skip to the end, get the bottom line, and then (if the writer's lucky), start in again at the top.

Even bad news should normally come early. You don't necessarily make it the first sentence: "You're fired." But that kind of news shouldn't follow a page and a half of the company's financial situation, either, should it?

Also, with bad news, tone becomes extremely important. You probably want to say something with a less rude tone than: "You're fired."

There are a number of ways to deliver the same message with a polite tone, and that message needs to be earlier rather than later.

First example: the auditors have come!

Suppose you've just had outside auditors look over your financial records. They've spent three months with access to all your files and all your people. Today they hand you their report. Do you want to plow through all their facts—

everything they examined—to find that your company looks great? Or that one of your division managers has been cheating? Wouldn't you rather have the conclusion up front?

For instance, consider these two good starts for audit reports (each with the bottom line up front):

> After three months of examining your records for the past year, we have found no major discrepancies.
>
> *or*
>
> After three months of examining your records for the past year, we have found the following:
>
> - Your marketing division is systematically hiding its losses each month—totaling $300,000 for the past 6 months alone.
>
> - The division manager and her assistant appear to be the only people involved.
>
> - There were no other major discrepancies.

Notice that starting with the main point doesn't mean saying only what you're going to cover: "This report tells you the results of the audit we've been conducting for the past three months." No, starting with the main point means telling what you found. Starting with only the topic simply isn't enough—just as a table of contents usually isn't enough to serve as the summary of a book.

Second example: the letter in the in-box

Don't you wonder, with every piece of paper in your in-box, "Does this ask me to *do* anything?" And don't you wish the writer would start with that—and then tell you why? Even with short memos and letters, most of us appreciate getting the main point early. For example, what if you're having a busy day as personnel director for your company, and this comes in from an employment agency:

> Dear Max:
>
> On December 15, I received a phone call from Mr. Jason Brown from Michigan, who was your director of sailing in the Saginaw school. Mr. Brown, who recently had a fine interview with us, has requested I contact you. He requests a letter of verification of employment, including confirmation of his job title and the duties he performed while in your school. According to Mr. Brown, he needs this to apply for a similar position in the Caribbean.
>
> I would appreciate your help in this matter.
>
> Sincerely,

What's the key sentence buried in that letter? It's the one asking for the verification of employment. You can find it without experiencing major frustration, but wouldn't you have preferred the request first—like this:

> Dear Max:
>
> Would you verify the employment of Mr. Jason Brown?
>
> Mr. Brown was your director of sailing in the Saginaw school [then give the rest of the details]. . . .
>
> Sincerely,

Better, isn't it?

Tip

For the next memo or letter you write, ask yourself, "Am I asking my reader to do anything?" If you are, try starting with that request—and put it in the form of a question (as in the example you just read).

Third example: where's that color printer???

At the beginning of the chapter, I mentioned that one reason writers put the main point last is to reenact how they learned something. In fact, I think that's probably the most common reason of all. Writers simply use the same order on paper in which events actually occurred.

Suppose, for example, you've been spending the last few days ordering a new printer for your office. Your boss says to you, "How about sending me a memo and letting me know where things stand." You might be tempted to organize your memo by chronology—the way things happened:

> On July 7, you asked me to order a color printer for our office. On that same day, I contacted Cameron Melton (our computer expert) and began coordinating our request with him. Cameron told me that we have the funds and that the kind of printer we want is on the authorized list. Therefore, Cameron gave us permission to make the buy.
>
> On July 9, I called the printer company and found out the exact price ($3,799). Later that day, I contacted Laura in purchasing. Together, Laura and I filled out the request for the printer.
>
> On July 11, Mackenzie okayed the order and sent it to the printer company.
>
> On July 14, I confirmed that the printer company received our order. The salesperson I spoke with said we will have the printer by 9:30 a.m. tomorrow.

Takes forever to get to the bottom line, doesn't it? You can see, though, that the writer simply followed the chronology of what happened, tracking the purchase step by step for the boss.

Writers are often tempted by chronological order. But what does the boss really want to know? Certainly not a blow-by-blow account of the process. Remember, the request was this: "Let me know where things stand." Keeping that in mind, let's try a different start:

> We'll be getting our color printer by 9:30 a.m. tomorrow. It will cost $3,799.
>
> Approval was simple: Cameron Melton (our computer expert) authorized it quickly. Laura (in purchasing) was very helpful preparing the order. Jason okayed the order and sent it out without incident.

Notice that the second memo gets right to the point: the printer is coming tomorrow. Notice also that the memo is much shorter. That often happens. When you begin with your main point, you're much less likely to put in anything irrelevant. In fact, you might not even need the second paragraph.

❖   ❖   ❖

So starting with the main point helps keep your reader on track—and *you* (the writer), too.

You'll learn more about organization in these chapters:

- Chapter 9, "Blueprint"
- Chapter 10, "Executive summary"

Now let's look at the last part of plain English: layout.

CHAPTER 4

Layout: adding visual impact

Bottom line

<u>*Show*</u> *your reader the underlying structure of your writing by using headings, lists, and other good techniques of white space.*

When I give presentations on writing, my audiences usually consider layout to be the most important topic I cover.

What is layout, anyway? On its simplest level, it is whatever goes into the "look" of the page: something that appears open and inviting probably has good layout; something that appears cluttered and *un*inviting probably has bad layout.

The look of a page is important, but we'll see that good layout has two other terrific advantages:

- Good layout shows the reader—visually—your organization.

- It also helps you—the writer—be organized in the first place.

Layout is much more than packaging a document: it is the driving force behind organization. People who are aware of the techniques of good layout almost always write with good organization.

In this chapter, I'll suggest three layout techniques:

- Use short paragraphs.
- Use headings.
- Use bullets and other lists.

These techniques are important at all times and *absolutely crucial* when the content of your writing is complex—as business writing often is.

Let's look at each of these techniques in more detail.

Use short paragraphs

Too often, the standard layout for business writing is wall-to-wall words. You've no doubt seen such pages. They look something like this (the gray part represents text):

One big paragraph—not very appealing, is it?

Now let's make the layout a *little* better by simply changing the shape of the words—arranging them into more paragraphs:

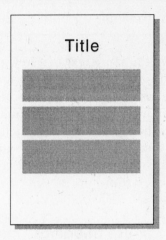

Looks better, doesn't it? And, of course, the paragraphs can be even shorter than these.

A question often comes up about this time: "But isn't a paragraph a paragraph? Can we start paragraphs just anywhere?"

We can't start paragraphs anywhere, but there are many options. The old (un)truism is this: "Each paragraph should represent a separate thought. Some thoughts take longer than others; therefore, some paragraphs may be very long."

To some extent, paragraphs do represent separate thoughts, but what is a "thought," anyway? Every sentence contains at least one thought and probably several. True, a new paragraph can signal the next major thought, but business writing has a better technique: headings.

If you use headings—and I highly recommend them—you can paragraph almost visually beneath them. The headings show the boundaries of the major "thoughts."

Also, think about newspapers—just how long are their paragraphs? Their paragraphs are short—because long paragraphs would be quite forbidding in narrow newspaper columns.

In fact, if you give the same text to a newspaper editor and to a textbook editor to divide into paragraphs, you'd get different results: the newspaper editor would give you many short paragraphs; the textbook editor would give you longer ones (because textbook columns are much wider). In other words, both editors would paragraph—to some extent—visually. And that's what I recommend you do, too. Now let's look at a related topic.

Use headings

Just using short paragraphs isn't good enough. You also need to *show* your organization—visually—to your readers. A good way to do that is with headings. Think of headings as "labels" for the parts of your document.

For example, the memo we just worked with has short paragraphs, but it doesn't have labels for the various parts. Let's improve it one more step by adding those "labels":

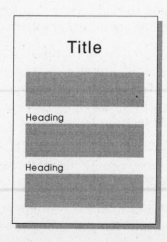

Tip

Make your headings actually communicate with your reader (such as "When will the new computers arrive?" instead of "computers"). And feel free to have more than one paragraph below a heading.

As you can see, headings are an important key to good business writing. They can also help you as a supervisor of writers. Suppose, for example, you're managing a large writing project. If you ask your people to use headings when they write, you know what you'll get? Not just headings, but organization, too. It's hard for people to use headings without being organized.

Headings are the "little thing that does the big thing": a technique of layout that forces good organization. At the very least, headings require people to arrange their document into blocks of information instead of scattering ideas throughout. Headings also often keep people from using a chronological organization, which, because it often buries the main point, usually isn't appropriate.

Use bullets and other indented lists

Headings are terrific—and so are indented lists. As you can tell, I seldom write more than a page or so without using them somewhere. Just as headings show organization for the blocks of information in a document, lists often show organization within paragraphs.

A quick example: the value of lists

Business writing often has lists in it somewhere, and organized writers use lists particularly often. A list is all right as part of the text of a paragraph, but it's usually more effective if it's indented.

For example, read this sentence:

> Three satellites are in geosynchronous orbit at 23,000 miles over the equator: Satellite I is at 55 degrees west longitude, Satellite II is at 70 degrees west longitude, and Satellite III is at 140 degrees west longitude.

Next, see how much better the layout is when we indent the list:

> Three satellites are in geosynchronous orbit at 23,000 miles over the equator:
>
> • Satellite I is at 55 degrees west longitude.
>
> • Satellite II is at 70 degrees west longitude.
>
> • Satellite III is at 140 degrees west longitude.

Indenting with bullets helps untangle that technical information.

A second example: bullets or numbers?

Here's another example—a set of instructions—that could benefit from indented lists:

> To set up this laptop computer, you must take the following steps. Push the dual latches mounted on top of the computer outward to release the top/monitor assembly. Move the top/monitor assembly to an oblique angle with the unit's base. Push the release switch on Disk Drive A away from you to release the drive.

This paragraph is well organized, but it doesn't look it. The problem is ineffective layout. So let's take a first step to improve the layout by using bullets—notice the difference already:

To set up this laptop computer, you must take the following steps:

- Push the dual latches mounted on top of the computer outward to release the top/monitor assembly.

- Move the top/monitor assembly to an oblique angle with the unit's base.

- Push the release switch on Disk Drive A away from you to release the drive.

The paragraph now isolates each step visually. Notice that all bulleted items begin the same way grammatically (in this case, with verbs). That's good. The grammatical term for that is "parallelism."

Even though the layout is much better for that paragraph (visually revealing the good organization that was already there), there's still a better way: a numbered list.

I suggest numbered lists when you're giving steps; otherwise, use bulleted lists (to give a unified look to the pages of your document). So my final solution would be a numbered list, like this:

To set up this laptop computer, you must take the following steps:

1. Push the dual latches mounted on top of the computer outward to release the top/monitor assembly.

2. Move the top/monitor assembly to an oblique angle with the unit's base.

3. Push the release switch on Disk Drive A away from you to release the drive.

❖　　　　❖　　　　❖

Do you see the advantage of good layout? It helps readers see a document's organization: the headings label the blocks of information; the indented lists isolate the facts, steps, arguments.

Even more important, good layout helps *produce* good organization. Writers who are aware of the techniques of good layout think about it *as* they write, not afterward. And as they write, they naturally form their ideas into blocks of information, and they isolate many of their facts, steps, and arguments into lists.

You'll learn more about layout in these chapters:

- Chapter 11, "Typefaces"
- Chapter 12, "Headings"
- Chapter 13, "Bullets"
- Chapter 14, "Graphics"

Now let's turn to the final chapter in this section. It puts everything together in a model.

CHAPTER 5

A model for writing

Bottom line

There's a simple model that can help you get started with a lot of your business writing.

This chapter presents a model you can use for much of your business writing—a "template" that will hold the ideas in many documents. These documents can be short (like memos) or long (like reports or even books).

If this sounds too good to be true, it isn't. I've used this model—or variations—many times, including for some of the most challenging and complex writing in government and business, writing involving complicated documents by auditors, lawyers, and accountants.

Basically, the model says to:

- start with your main point
- organize your writing into blocks of information
- label those blocks with headings so your readers can see where blocks start and end

The model is simple. And it seems obvious. But how often do you see writing that actually follows it? Once you try it, you'll see how often you can use it.

It's simple and effective!

A model for writing

First, let's look at an illustration of what the model *isn't:*

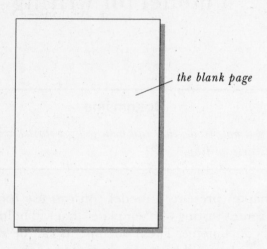

the blank page

The blank page! Now let's look at the model:

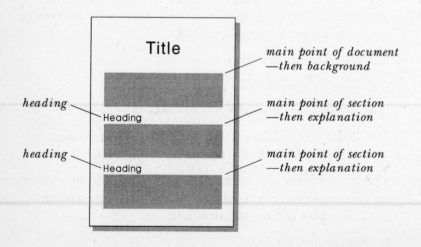

And here's an explanation of the model:

1. Begin with your main point: whatever you want your reader to do or understand.

2. Organize your content into sections—or blocks—of related information. Those blocks don't have to be single paragraphs—they could be pages long (broken into short paragraphs, of course).

3. Label each of those blocks with a heading. Use sub-headings, too, if the blocks are long.

4. Try to start each block by stating its main point. For example, if your heading is a question, begin the block by answering that question.

5. And use details—sometimes in bulleted lists—to support that main point.

Simple, isn't it?

The model in action

Let's apply the model. Here, as an example, is the beginning of a memo:

This memo asks for your authorization to rent three computers for $900 total cost.

We've ordered three personal computers to work on the Laredo project, but the supplier can't get them to us until June 1. Because we must start the project sooner, we need to rent other computers in the meantime. This memo gives you the details.

Why are our new computers late?
The manufacturer had trouble with defective computer chips. As a result. . . . [The memo then continues with

more explanation in this paragraph and more sections
with headings.]

Notice that:

- The first paragraph is the main point of the document: I want you to pay $900 to rent computers.

- There are headings to label the blocks of information
  in the body of the document. This example, which
  shows only the beginning of the memo, has the heading, "Why are our new computers late?"

- The first sentence after the heading is the main point
  of the section: the manufacturer had trouble with
  computer chips.

You can see this model can help untangle complex information for the reader—and for the writer. If you aim for
this model when you begin writing, starting will be easier,
and you'll be more organized.

Does this model seem mechanical? Yes, it is. Too mechanical? I doubt it. The content of business writing can become
extraordinarily complex; at the same time, readers are
often busy. A mechanical organization is a blessing for a
busy reader (for busy writers, too).

Think about yourself around April 15 each year. What
kind of organization do you want for the instructions on
filling out your income tax forms? If you're like me, you
want the organization to be *absolutely clear*—with no ambi-
guity whatsoever.

Does the model work all the time?

No—not all the time.

It works especially well for busy readers who want to get
information as quickly as possible and then move on to

something else. It works for people who *have* to read whatever you're writing and want the writing to be as painless as possible.

It doesn't work as well when you need to engage readers creatively and hold their attention with an entertaining style or innovative organization. Frankly, most people enjoy that kind of writing off the job but don't enjoy it on the job. They see the creative part as a waste of time (I don't, but I've found I'm in the minority).

Again, think of yourself as a reader: how much of the writing you read could benefit by following this model?

Does the model work for technical writing?

Yes, the model works *especially* well for technical, complex writing. In fact, the more complex the writing is, the more important this model is for the reader. But just because the model works for complex writing doesn't mean it isn't suited for simple explanations and recommendations, too. The example in this chapter—about renting a computer— is relatively simple, and the model serves it well.

Do you need to follow all parts of the model?

No, you don't need to follow all parts of the model all the time. For example, sometimes you might want to give the reader a little background before you can make your main point—either for the entire document or part of it.

You must still be careful, though, to keep the background to a minimum before you get to the point. Remember: readers know how to skip ahead.

When I have a lot of background to cover, I try to give the minimum up front, then state the main point, then add background if necessary. But a funny thing happens when I get the main point up front: I find I need much less background than I thought.

So keep the model in mind *before* and *as* you write. It's simple and effective.

❖   ❖   ❖

You've now read about each of the key parts of writing in plain English:

- style: writing the way you talk
- organization: getting to the point
- layout: adding visual impact

The next three sections tell you more about each of those parts.

MORE ABOUT
STYLE

CHAPTER 6

Passive voice

Bottom line

Use active voice—unless you have a <u>strong</u> reason to use passive.

This chapter attacks the most important villain of readability in business and technical writing: passive voice.

If you've heard one outcry against bad business and government writing, it's "Too much passive voice!" That's a good outcry, because bureaucratic writers significantly overuse it. Passive voice isn't always bad, but lots of it absolutely kills readability.

What is passive voice?

Identifying passive voice is simple. Just go through these two steps:

1. Look for a form of the verb *to be*. Here's the complete list: *am, are, is, was, were, be, been, being.*

2. Now look for a past participle. These are easy to identify: they normally end in *-ed* or *-en*. Examples: *carried, taken*. Note: There are a few irregular verbs that have past participles that don't end in *-ed* or *-en*: *held, made, kept,* etc. You'll soon get the hang of identifying them.

If both parts are present, you have passive voice. Here's an example:

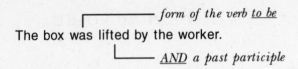

Here are some other examples of verbs in the passive voice:

has *been* fitt*ed*

could have *been* tak*en*

were writt*en*

is done (irregular verb)

are kept (irregular verb)

Notice that you can always add a prepositional phrase beginning with *by* to passive sentences:

The suit has been fitted *by the tailor*.

The report is kept *by the analysts*.

Easy enough, isn't it? So just look for:

- a form of the verb *to be*
- *and* a past participle

If you have both, you have a verb that's passive. And because you have a passive verb, there will always be a slot for a prepositional phrase beginning with *by*.

So where does the name "passive" come from?

Sentences with passive voice have a subject that's "passive." That is, the subject isn't doing whatever the verb says. It's not the actor; instead, it's acted upon.

In this sentence, for example, the subject ("the ball") is passive. It's acted upon:

subject
Passive voice: The ball was tossed by Elizabeth.
acted upon **ACTOR**

Now let's turn things around and make the sentence active:

subject
Active voice: Elizabeth tossed the ball.
ACTOR *acted upon*

The subject ("Elizabeth") is now active. It's doing what the verb says: tossing.

What's the difference: voice and tense?

Some people confuse passive voice and past tense. They think they have to use passive voice because something happened in the past. No. *Passive* voice and *past* tense may sound alike, but they're completely different.

Here's a verb with passive voice and past tense:

The file cabinet was moved.

And here's proof we don't need to use passive voice for something that happened in the past:

The contractor moved the file cabinet.

That sentence is still past tense but now in active voice.

Voice, as we've seen, refers to whether or not the subject is the actor in the sentence. *Tense*, on the other hand, simply refers to the time an action takes place (past, present, future). So you can have any combination of voice and tense.

What's the matter with passive voice?

Passive voice isn't wrong, but it often causes problems. That's because it often leaves out information that the reader needs. Let me explain how that happens—usually unconsciously by the writer. Remember I said that passive sentences always have a slot for a prepositional phrase beginning with *by*?

> The policy has been approved by the CEO.

> or

> The policy has been approved.

In the first sentence, the words in the *by* phrase (showing the actor) are actually there; in the second, they aren't there, but there's a place—a slot—for them. Both sentences, of course, are passive.

Too often, passive sentences in business writing are like the second sentence: they leave out the *by* phrase (and, consequently, the actor). Sometimes you, the reader, can guess who the actor is; sometimes you can't. For example, look at this sentence:

> When a computer file has *been created*, it must *be moved* to the remote node.

Sounds simple, even though it's passive, doesn't it? But what does it mean? Notice that it has left out both *by* phases (and both actors):

> When a computer file has been created [by ???], it must be moved [by ???] to the remote node.

So we have to guess who—or what—the actors are: Is the *user* creating the computer file? Probably—but we're guessing. And who is moving the computer file? The user? The system administrator? The system itself? Unless we already know what this writer is talking about, we must guess.

Well, this sentence came from a writer I was working with. Here's what he wrote when I asked him to put the sentence into active voice:

> When a *user* creates a computer file, the *system* must move it to the remote node.

Just check your in-box. Find a piece of writing that's hard to read. And then notice how many passives leave out the *by* phrase—and leave you guessing who is doing the action.

Why do people write passive voice?

One reason people write passive voice is to *intentionally* leave out the actor. For example, timid bosses wouldn't want to write this sentence:

> I have decided everybody must work this weekend.

The actor is *I*—who may seem pretty exposed to gripes and other criticism from the people who can't go sailing or skiing during the weekend. So some bureaucrats, to avoid responsibility, tend to put such a sentence in passive voice and then eliminate the *by* prepositional phrase:

> It has been determined ~~by me~~ that you must work this weekend.

Now, through the magic of passive voice, the boss is in the clear. After all, who can find the subject of that sentence—"It"—to gripe to?

But this reason—avoiding responsibility—actually accounts for only a small percentage of the sentences in passive voice. After all, only a few key sentences in any document are ones in which people must accept or avoid responsibility.

A second reason people write passively is that they try to avoid using personal pronouns like *we* and *you*. However, unless they use personal pronouns, passive voice is the natural result.

So pronouns are the key. In fact, bosses who say, "Write in plain English, but don't use any personal pronouns," are like home builders who say, "Build me a nice house, but—hey—I don't like hammers, so don't use them." Hard to build a house without hammers, and hard to write plain English without pronouns.

And a third reason people write passively? They just do. They start in passive voice and then just stay in passive voice. Without much effort at all, they could easily have written the same ideas actively.

Is passive voice ever all right?

Of course. At least three times:

- when you don't know the actor ("John was murdered.")
- when the actor is unimportant to the point you're making ("The senator was reelected.")
- when the emphasis is clearly not on the actor but on the acted upon ("What happened to the little girl? *The little girl* was rescued.")

So don't think of passive voice as always bad. Think of it as putting unnecessary strain on the reader. Use passive when you need to—but be careful of overusing it. Seldom have readers suffered because writers overused *active* voice.

Tip

Work hard to use active voice. Try to use passive only as a relatively uncommon exception.

✤   ✤   ✤

Is writing active voice worth the effort? Absolutely! It can make a dramatic impact on the readability of your writing. In fact, if you habitually write passive voice, I can almost guarantee that your readers have been skimming in frustration and confusion.

Do you want to find out if you're writing passive voice? Take some of your recent business writing and circle all the passives on one full page. If you find only two or three, you're doing fine. If, on the other hand, you find many more . . .

Some of today's grammar checkers can tell you what percentage of your verbs are in passive voice. I average under 3% in this book. You should definitely be under 10% for most of your writing.

Now let's turn to another serious problem of business writing: abstractness. It's almost as serious a problem as passive voice.

CHAPTER 7

Abstractness

Bottom line

Keep your reader from guessing what you mean—by using examples, brief stories, and comparisons.

This chapter helps you conquer another villain of readability: abstractness. Let's begin by defining it.

What is abstract writing?

Abstract writing is so general that readers constantly have to guess what it means. If I stopped there, that sentence would be abstract—you'd have to guess what *I* mean. So let's consider an example. Here's an abstract sentence:

As a property manager, I sometimes find strange things.

It's hard to picture exactly what the writer means. Things can be "strange" in different ways. We're left, to some extent, to guess exactly what the writer means by that word.

As a result, the sentence isn't memorable. By memorable, I don't mean deathless prose such as "Give me liberty or give me death!" I simply mean something we can remember by the time we finish the page. Abstract sentences don't pass the "memorable" test.

So abstract writing is writing that is ambiguous and hard for us to picture.

The opposite of "abstract" is "concrete." So let's move beyond the abstract sentence I just showed you by adding a concrete illustration:

> As a property manager, I sometimes find strange things. At one property, I found two people living in an electrical room (the room housing electrical meters). They worked at the property and lived in the closet . . . mostly trying to avoid a long commute.

The illustration helps us visualize what the writer means by "strange." As a result, the passage has moved from abstract to concrete. It isn't deathless prose, but we'll probably remember it well after we turn the page. The concreteness helps it become more memorable.

Abstract writing, then, is so vague that it asks us to stop reading and guess what it means. Normally we don't do that. Instead, we just keep reading, hoping for something better in the next sentence or the next paragraph. If there isn't anything better, we might just go to lunch.

Even if we make educated guesses to figure out the abstract writing, we can't be sure we've gotten the author's intended meaning. That's why professional writers take the guesswork out by supplying the missing information.

How can you be more concrete?

Concreteness is crucial to good writing. The rest of the chapter looks at these three ways to be more concrete:

- Use quick examples.
- Tell brief stories.
- Make comparisons.

Use quick examples

A quick example is normally fairly short—from a word to a couple of sentences. Here are three:

> As a loan officer, I will not hesitate to hold up an application of a member whose salary I question. *For example, I would be suspicious of someone who is eighteen and makes $50,000.*

•　　　•　　　•

> I am responsible for making sure the computer system is running smoothly every day. If there are any problems—*such as a database running out of space*—I am called to fix it.

•　　　•　　　•

> We answer over 100 questions a day from federal employees about our program to offer them incentives to resign. *For example, employees often call to find out if they are eligible. We received one call from a wife whose husband had taken the buyout. She had put up with him at home for a week and had had enough. She wanted his agency to take him back!*

Lists are another good place for quick examples. For instance, auditors try to find out whether things are going well within an organization. If they find something wrong, that something is a "finding." This list tells auditors what a report of a finding should cover:

> These are the five elements of a finding you must cover in your report:
>
> 1. condition
>
> 2. cause
>
> 3. criteria
>
> 4. effect
>
> 5. recommendation

Abstract. Now for the concrete. Let's put in some quick examples:

> These are the five elements of a finding you must cover in your report:
>
> 1. *Condition*. Example: The nurses don't record the medicine they give their patients.
>
> 2. *Cause*. Example: The nursing staff is 42% short of people, leaving little time for nurses to both give the medicine and record that they've given it.
>
> 3. *Criteria*. Example: Hospital Regulation 213.4 says that whoever gives medicine must record that fact.
>
> 4. *Effect*. Example: Patients could die or have worsened conditions if they receive too much or too little medicine.
>
> 5. *Recommendation*. Example: Counsel all nurses and require supervisors to monitor the records.

You certainly noticed that the concrete version is longer. That's true. But longer is not necessarily worse. The real issue is, "Which version communicates more efficiently to the reader?" Sometimes more writing is better than less.

You may wonder when you should use quick examples. The answer: whenever your reader won't understand the abstract version alone. Professional writers use them frequently.

Tip _____

A good suggestion for supervisors is to tell your people to use lots of these two transitions (or words like them): <u>for instance</u> and <u>for example</u>. The result will almost always be more concreteness. And concreteness translates to information that readers remember.

Tell brief stories

We all love stories. What's our reaction when a speaker says, "Let me tell you what happened last Saturday evening"? Our ears perk up, and we suddenly pay attention.

The same thing happens to readers—a story perks them up. Consider this one:

> Part of my job is to help low-income families. For example, a family of three (soon to be four) moved from a homeless shelter to an apartment. The only things they brought with them were the clothes on their backs.
>
> The manager of the property asked me to help this family with utilities, clothing, furniture, and food. So I called the electric and phone companies to give them information about the family.
>
> Once the companies processed the information, the electricity and phone began to work. The next thing was to find clothes and furniture. The family and I went to the Salvation Army. We found some good quality clothes and good pieces of furniture to take back to their apartment.
>
> Finally, I showed them where the nearest grocery store was and how to use food stamps.

See how the story helps make something abstract—helping others—more memorable? Sometimes, for an important point, the extra words a story requires are well worth the reader's time.

Make comparisons

If there's one technique of concreteness that separates amateurs from professionals, it's that professionals tend to use many comparisons.

However, comparisons have a plus and a minus:

- *The plus.* A good comparison will probably be the most memorable part of a piece of writing.

- *The minus.* A good comparison is hard to think of.

Nevertheless, many people have thought of excellent ones. John D. MacDonald, a famous novelist, used comparisons often in his writing. Here's one from *The Dreadful Lemon Sky* telling us about news stories:

> But a news story is a fragile thing. *It is like a hot air balloon. It needs a constant additive of more hot air in the form of new revelations, new actions, new suspicions. Without this the air cools, the big bag wrinkles, sighs, settles to the ground, and disappears.*

We know that comparisons appear in novels, but do they appear in business writing? Yes. Here's a good one about "client-serving computing":

> A common use for client-serving computing is for processing large amounts of data. For example, if you need to produce a huge personnel report, you can have a powerful computer come up with the data for the report (doing the number crunching and sorting), and you can put the data on a less powerful computer to format the report. *In this case, it's like digging a ditch with a backhoe to dig up the heavy dirt and then using shovels to even out the edges of the hole.*

✢   ✢   ✢

So check your writing for abstractness. Are there places you could add quick examples? Brief stories? Comparisons? Your writing may grow a bit longer, but it will probably communicate much better.

Now let's look at the final chapter on style: punctuation. It can make a big difference in your writing.

CHAPTER 8

Punctuation

Bottom line

Use colons, dashes, semicolons, question marks, and other punctuation to replace the voice inflection and hand gestures we use when we talk.

Punctuation has intimidated brave men and women for years. Yet it's not that hard—really. This chapter simplifies some rules and makes them easier to learn.

How often is punctuation important when you write? The answer: every time. So take a few minutes now to expand your arsenal. There's no need to spend the rest of your life restricted to only the period, the comma, and the colon introducing a list.

This chapter gives a few new ways to look at colons, dashes, and semicolons.

Why is punctuation important?

Imagine, if you will, a string of words with no punctuation whatsoever:

xx xxxx xxx xxxxx xx x xxxxxxxxx xxxx xx x xxxxxxx xxxx
xx x xxxx xxxxxx xxx xxxxxx xx xxxxxxxxxx xxx xxxx
xxxxxx xxx xxxx xxxx xx xxxxxxxxxxx

There's a misconception that someone who is good at punctuation simply knows what punctuation mark should go where: a comma here, a semicolon there, a period at the end.

However, for someone who is good at punctuation, the words come out differently than for someone who is not. People who understand commas, semicolons, periods— and especially colons, dashes, and question marks—produce entirely different sentence structures from people who are not good at punctuation.

The result? Better sentences that have the emphasis—and ideas—in just the right places.

So don't think of punctuation as a way to go *wrong* (as a way to make mistakes). Instead, think of punctuation as a way to go *right*—as a way to say just what you mean in the best way possible.

Please note: This chapter gives you only a few of the most common and useful rules for colons, dashes, and semicolons. If you follow these rules, you will produce correct punctuation. But don't "correct" other people's writing just because they don't follow the rules here. There are other correct ways I don't include. (For a more complete look at punctuation, see any of the various handbooks on writing.)

The colon

General definition of the colon

The colon is an extremely useful mark of punctuation. Think of it as an "arrow" that comes at the end of a complete sentence, pointing to some more useful information about what you just said. The colon can "point" to a word, to a list, to a sentence, even to a series of sentences or paragraphs.

Rules for the colon

1. Use a colon (after a complete sentence) to point to a single word:

   • He started the business for one reason: money.

2. Use a colon (after a complete sentence) to point to a list:

   • He started the business for three reasons: adventure, fame, and money.

3. Use a colon (after a complete sentence) to point to another complete sentence:

   • He had always been a thrill-seeker: he once climbed the northwest face of Half Dome.

4. Use a colon (after a complete sentence) to point to a series of sentences or paragraphs:

   • He started the business for three reasons: He wanted adventure. He wanted fame. He wanted money.

Notice in each of these cases that the part after the colon receives emphasis. For instance, what's the difference between these two sentences?

   • He started the business because he wanted money.

   • He started the business for one reason: money.

Emphasis! The word *money* in the second sentence seems to have a spotlight on it.

Now—which is the better sentence? We can't say, can we? It depends on context and how much emphasis we want to give to *money*.

But who is the better writer: the one who can write both kinds of sentences or the one who can write only the one without the colon? Probably the one who writes both kinds is better because that person has more tools to control emphasis.

Now let's look at another important mark for plain English—the dash.

The dash

General definition of the dash

Like the colon, the dash is an extremely useful mark of punctuation. It tells the reader that you are saying "something more" about what you just said—an example, an elaboration, a contradiction, whatever.

Handbooks once discouraged the dash as too informal for business writing; today we see the old books as too formal for plain English. Now the dash is a fully accredited mark of punctuation.

Tip

Use a dash in the next thing you write. If you haven't been using a dash in your business writing before, you'll find it to be remarkably handy for emphasizing your important ideas.

Rules for the dash

1. Use a dash as you would a colon: as an "arrow" that comes at the end of a complete sentence, pointing to some more useful information about what you just said. Notice that the dash gives a slightly more informal feel to the sentence than a colon does:

   • He started the business for one reason—money.

   • He started the business for three reasons—adventure, fame, and money.

- He had always been a thrill-seeker—he once climbed the northwest face of Half Dome.

Normally you shouldn't use the dash to point to a series of sentences or paragraphs.

2. Use a pair of dashes (one on each side) to set off useful information in the middle of a sentence:

- He robbed the bank—the one just around the corner—for the sheer adventure.

The sentence is, "He robbed the bank for the sheer adventure." The phrase "the one just around the corner" is in the middle of the sentence.

Question: What three marks could you put around that phrase?

Answer: a set of commas, a set of dashes, or a set of parentheses.

The difference? Dashes add emphasis to the phrase, commas give standard emphasis, and parentheses treat it like a whispered aside.

3. Use a dash (even where you might have no other punctuation) to emphasize the last idea in a sentence:

- He robbed the bank—for adventure, notoriety, and greed.

- He robbed the bank for adventure, notoriety—and greed.

Again, you can see the effect the dash has on emphasis.

The semicolon

General definition of the semicolon

The semicolon is more formal than the colon and the dash. Professional writers today tend to use it much less than writers of several decades ago did.

Some people think of the semicolon as a "strong comma"—
something between a comma and a period. That's true,
but it's not the whole story.

The semicolon also has to separate equal grammatical units—an
independent clause from another independent clause, or
a dependent clause from another dependent clause, or a
phrase from a phrase. The semicolon does not separate
unequal units—like an *in*dependent clause from a *de*pen-
dent clause.

In other words, think of the semicolon as a kind of "pivot":
one idea is on this side of the semicolon; another idea is
on that side of it. And on each side of the pivot point is a
similar grammatical unit.

Rules for the semicolon

1. Use a semicolon to join two (or more) complete sentences to show that those sentences are closely related.

   • In spring, the blossoms are beautiful on the apple trees;
     in autumn, the apples are a nuisance on the lawn.

You may wonder how the semicolon is different from a
colon or dash, which can also separate two sentences.
The difference has to do with the second sentence, the
one after the colon, dash, or semicolon. For the colon
and dash, the second sentence is usually an example or
elaboration; for the semicolon, the second sentence is
usually a similar or opposite idea (as in this sentence). If
this seems a bit fuzzy, you're right: there aren't clear
rights and wrongs.

Now here's another example of a semicolon separating
two sentences:

   • The rock climber forgot to bring his rope and pitons;
     however, he remembered to bring the food.

Some people think a word like *however* should always have a semicolon before it. No—the word *however* can move from the beginning of the independent clause to the middle or end of it. The semicolon still stays between the independent clauses—thus separating similar grammatical units:

- The rock climber forgot to bring his rope and pitons; he remembered, however, to bring the food.

2. Use a semicolon to separate items in series if any item in the series has commas in it.

Here's a sentence with incorrect punctuation—notice the confusion:

- *Confusing:* Many stars from the carnival were there: the ringmaster, Harpo and Groucho, the clowns, Feline, the lion tamer, Ursula, the bear, and, fortunately, Zorro, the bear tamer.

Now let's add semicolons—notice how much easier the sentence is to understand:

- *Correct:* Many stars from the carnival were there: the ringmaster; Harpo and Groucho, the clowns; Feline, the lion tamer; Ursula, the bear; and, fortunately, Zorro, the bear tamer.

But bullets would be better, wouldn't they?

Experiment with these marks and with those you already know how to use: parentheses, question marks, and italicizing for emphasis. The results will be dramatic.

MORE ABOUT
ORGANIZATION

CHAPTER 9

Blueprint

Bottom line

Tell your readers, up front, the structure of your document.

This chapter will cover three topics:

- What is a blueprint?
- Do you always need a blueprint?
- How can you write a good blueprint?

What is a blueprint?

A blueprint is simply a brief outline of what you'll cover. Here's an example:

> From my point of view, we may classify risks as:
>
> - noncommercial
> - political
> - financial
>
> Let's look more closely at these.

As a reader, you now know the structure of the document you've just begun to read: you know it has three parts, you know what they are, and you know the order they should appear in.

As a writer, you usually want your reader to be comfortable with the structure of your document. That way, your reader can spend more energy concentrating on its content.

A blueprint is especially important for documents longer than a page or so. Think of your document as a trip for your reader. The blueprint is like a road map—saying what various stops you're going to make along the way: "First, we'll look at noncommercial risks, then move on to political risks, and finally end with financial risks."

Tip

Use a heading for each section of your document that you've blueprinted. For example, you could have a heading for your discussion of each of the three risks: noncommercial, political, and financial. The headings then become like road signs for your reader's "trip."

Let's look at another blueprint, this from *Consumer Reports,* telling us how to buy a new car:

> Before you think of shopping for a car, do your homework. Approach your car-shopping methodically, in the following sequence:
>
> • Narrow your choices of cars and equipment.
>
> • Find out what the dealer paid the factory for the car.
>
> • Shop more than one dealer.
>
> • Keep the transaction as simple and straightforward as possible.
>
> Let's examine each step in detail.

As a reader, you now know, without guessing, the structure of the document you've just begun to read.

Do you always need a blueprint?

No. If your document is short, telling its structure may seem too mechanical.

Another time a blueprint may seem too mechanical is when your document has many parts. Suppose, for example, it has nine sections. Readers normally don't want to read through a list of the nine topics you're going to cover. On the other hand, a document with nine sections can get confusing, can't it?

So I suggest using an implied blueprint: "I'll cover the nine issues in the case, starting with the most important one." Your reader now knows the structure of your document. You've given the number of "stops" on the trip but not the lengthy list of their names.

And what if you can't give a blueprint of your document? That means you probably haven't organized it into clear blocks of information. Very occasionally that's okay for a document. Most times, though, busy readers will become confused and start skimming.

How can you write a good blueprint?

Here are some tips for writing good blueprints:

- Consider highlighting (such as using bullets) to emphasize the blueprint list.

- Put a sentence after the blueprint telling your readers you're going to say more about each item ("Let's examine each step in detail"). That way your readers know they've read not just a list—but a list of the topics you're about to elaborate on.

- Be sure that the headings in the body of your document match the key words in your blueprint. For example, the first heading in the *Consumer Reports* article on buying a car is "Narrow Your Choices." The heading helps reinforce the structure of the document.

❖   ❖   ❖

As I mentioned in Chapter 5, this may all seem mechanical. But when we're reading complex information, a clear structure is a huge benefit. The blueprint helps your reader understand that structure.

CHAPTER 10

Executive summary

Bottom line

For longer documents, summarize up front—including your bottom line.

An executive summary is like an "elevator briefing." Here's what I mean: Suppose you get on an elevator with your boss, who asks, "How's your project going?" You need to finish your answer by the time you get to the fourth floor. What would you say?

You'd probably give a quick, bottom-line summary. And what's effective for a busy person on an elevator is also effective for a busy person sitting at a desk. An executive summary, then, is a quick, bottom-line summary. The difference from an elevator briefing is that the executive summary is in writing.

An executive summary normally is at the beginning of a document. And it's normally short.

In this chapter, let's consider these questions:

- Who reads an executive summary?
- How long should an executive summary be?
- Is there a structure for an executive summary?
- What are some cautions?

Who reads an executive summary?

The answer seems obvious: executives, of course. That's true—but not the whole story.

The main reason for an executive summary is often to let a busy executive, usually a highly placed boss, read the summary instead of the document itself. If the executive summary is good, the executive can learn all the important bottom-line information up front.

However, there are other important audiences:

- *Other people who are too busy to read the document.* The top boss may not be the only one who doesn't have time for the entire document but still needs the quick bottom line. Staff members, for example, may have such a need.

- *People wondering if they ought to read the document.* Without an executive summary, the only way to know if a document is relevant is to read it. But with a well-designed executive summary, the decision becomes much easier.

- *People who will read the entire document anyway.* Let's face it: *all* of us appreciate an executive summary. If we have to read the entire document anyway, the executive summary provides context—all the bottom-line information right there at the beginning.

How long should an executive summary be?

The traditional answer is "one page." However, I've seen good ones that are three pages long (for 40-page documents). And I've seen other good ones that are only a paragraph.

Is there a general structure for an executive summary?

I think so:

- Executive summaries should usually begin with the bottom line. That three-page executive summary I just mentioned had the bottom line up front. In a way, the beginning was like a summary within a summary—a good way to begin. What if the bottom line doesn't make sense at the very beginning? Then I'd give the *minimum* background necessary to understand the bottom line first—followed immediately by the bottom line. Normally a sentence or two of background is enough.

- The middle part of the summary should be "skimmable." That is, it should probably have headings and bullets. Key illustrations are also entirely appropriate.

- The end of the summary should explain the structure of the main report to the reader. Think of this as a blueprint of what's to follow.

Now let's look at an executive summary. This is the summary of a report to the head of a chain of shoe stores, urging a particular way for the stores to buy shoes.

Main recommendation
This report recommends we buy most of our shoes from wholesalers during visits to the wholesalers' warehouses.

The problem
Now we buy shoes from the following sources:

- catalogs
- sales calls
- shows
- visits to wholesalers

The result? Too often we have shoes cluttering our store—shoes in strange colors, styles, and sizes that we have trouble selling. Worse, we often don't have the right colors, styles, and sizes to make sales.

That's why I recommend visiting wholesalers. That way, we can see the actual colors and styles we purchase, and we can check for quality and fit. Then we won't be stuck with shoes we can't sell.

What this report covers
In this report, I discuss the advantages and disadvantages of each way we buy shoes. And then I explain why the last way—visits to wholesalers—is better than each of the other ways.

You can see how valuable this summary would be to a reader about to read the lengthy report.

Tip

Spend lots of time getting the words just right in your executive summary. Remember that more people probably read the executive summary than any other part of a report. The summary should show the <u>most</u> crafting—not the least.

What are some cautions?

Too often, writers forget the purpose of an executive summary—something to read *instead of* the entire report. As a result, two problems sometimes occur.

Sometimes the summary doesn't give the bottom line. The summary to the head of the shoe stores *does* give it: buy from wholesalers. However, what if the summary said only something like this?

> This report recommends ways to buy our shoes. These
> are the sources the report considers:
>
> - catalogs
> - sales calls
> - shows
> - visits to wholesalers
>
> The report examines each of these in detail and then
> makes a recommendation.

You can see that this version simply announces the topic; it doesn't give the recommendation (buy from wholesalers). Readers of executive summaries *especially* want the recommendation—that's often the main reason they're looking at the report.

A second problem with executive summaries is that they may use unfamiliar jargon. Often reports—especially technical ones—take care to define new terms before they use those terms later in the report. Poor executive summaries sometimes include those same terms—without defining them.

There's a great temptation to use the undefined terminology in the summary because defining it might take up valuable space. That's true, but the answer is not to use the unfamiliar terminology anyway. The answer is to find plain English equivalents so you can talk in general terms.

For example, suppose I'm writing a report on types of writing needs for people in business. I wouldn't use the term *syntactic fluency* in the executive summary, even though that term might be crucial in the report, itself. Instead, for the summary, I'd use a plain English paraphrase: "help people learn to vary their sentence structure." I'll wait to use the technical term until I've defined it in the report, itself.

And a third problem with executive summaries is that inexperienced writers sometimes create them by cutting and pasting sentences and paragraphs from the report. The resulting summaries tend to be fragmented and incoherent.

✣   ✣   ✣

Now on to some ways to improve layout—which computers have made not only possible, but fun!

MORE ABOUT
LAYOUT

CHAPTER 11

Typefaces

Bottom line

Choose your typefaces carefully. The right ones can mean whether your readers pick up your document in the first place.

We have incredible power over the look of our documents—more power than entire print shops of a decade ago. The trick is to use that power effectively for conveying the message. The goal of this chapter is to show you how.

These are my suggestions:

- Prefer serif type for your main text.
- Prefer sans serif type for most headings.
- Choose your type size carefully.
- Be careful with full justification.
- Restrict bold to titles and headings.
- Use italics to emphasize text within paragraphs.

After explaining these suggestions, I'll finish with some sample typefaces for you to compare.

Prefer serif type for your main text

There are many ways to classify typefaces, but the most common is whether or not they have serifs. Can you see the difference between the letters in the left and right columns?

T   T

L   L

The letters on the left have small lines at the ends of the strokes. Those are "serifs." The letters on the right don't have those small lines and are "sans serif." (*Sans* is French for "without.")

I recommend serif type for your main text (basically, the text for your paragraphs—excluding titles, headings, etc.).

Why? Simply because that's what we're used to. In the United States, an overwhelming number of documents use serif typefaces for the main text. Just check the newspapers, magazines, and books you read. You'll see serif almost all the time except for headings and titles and other occasional uses.

So using serif type for your main text is a standard. That doesn't mean that's the right way to do things—just the common way. Professionals often do creative and effective things that violate standards.

So can you.

Here are some common serif typefaces (all 12-point type):

New Baskerville: abcdefghijklmnop
New Century Schoolbook: abcdefghijklmnop
Palatino: abcdefghijklmnop
Times New Roman: abcdefghijklmnop

Prefer sans serif type for most headings

Sans serif type makes a nice heading—it contrasts with the serif type in your main text. Because of that contrast, sans serif type also works nicely for block quotations, indented examples, captions, and sidebars.

Here are some common sans serif typefaces (all 12-point type):

Arial: abcdefghijklmnop
Avant Garde: abcdefghijklmnop
Helvetica: abcdefghijklmnop
Optima: abcdefghijklmnop

If you're wondering why Avant Garde looks big and Optima looks small—yet both are in 12-point type—the next section explains why.

Choose your type size carefully

When I ask people what type size is appropriate for the main text in their business writing, almost all say, immediately, "12 point." A better answer, though, is, "It depends." And it depends on these three things:

- How long are your lines?
- How wide is your type?
- How tall are the basic lower case letters?

How long are your lines?

Have you ever wondered why we can read small type fairly easily in a newspaper but not in a standard business letter? That's because the length of the line on a page is almost as important as the size of the type. We can read 10-point type in a newspaper column that's two inches wide. However, if we tried that in a column six inches wide, we'd be squinting.

Most business writing is in a single column on an 8½ by 11 inch sheet of paper. With normal margins, the length of your line will be about six inches or so. For that length, you'll probably want to use a type size that's 12 or 12½ or 13 points. To decide which, you need to consider the next two topics.

How wide is your type?

Have you ever noticed that 12-point type sometimes looks smaller than at other times? Actually, in a way, it *is* smaller! That's because typesetters measure the size of type only by its *height,* not by its width, yet both affect how large or small the type appears to us. Typesetters measure the size of type in points (1/72 inch):

} *point size*

When we say a type size is 12 points, we essentially mean that the vertical distance from the top of the tallest character to the bottom of the lowest is 12 points.

But some typefaces have letters that are *wide*—which point size doesn't measure. As a result, these typefaces look big for their point size. Other typefaces are narrow—and look small for their point size.

You can see that effect when you look at the alphabet in two different typefaces. Notice that the sample of Times New Roman takes less space across the page than New Baskerville does:

Times New Roman: abcdefghijklmnopqrstuvwxyz
New Baskerville: abcdefghijklmnopqrstuvwxyz

Both samples are in 12-point type, but Times New Roman is more narrow—or *compressed*—than is New Baskerville. The difference may seem slight, but if you print an entire page of each typeface, you'll instantly see the differences:

- The compressed typeface—Times New Roman—seems smaller.

- The compressed typeface also seems to make the page darker and sometimes more cluttered.

Tip

To find out how compressed or expanded your typefaces are, simply do what I just did: type the entire alphabet for several typefaces and compare them.

With a compressed typeface, then, I recommend that you use 12½ or 13 points. But before you make your decision, you need to consider the final topic: the height of the lower case letters.

How tall are the basic lower case letters?

As I just discussed, one reason type can look small is that it is compressed. Another reason is that the basic lower case letters may be short. For the sake of explanation, let's say that basic lower case letters include:

- letters not having ascenders or descenders, like *a, c, o,* and *x,* to name a few

- the parts of letters—like *b, d, p*—not including the ascenders and descenders (just the bowls of the *b,* the *d,* and the *p,* for example)

Within a particular typeface, all basic lower case letters are about the same height. But the basic lower case letters in one typeface may be much taller or shorter than those in another typeface.

For example, believe it or not, both of these next examples are the same overall point size—as the lines across the top and bottom show:

$$\underline{\overline{\text{dpx}} \ \text{dpx}}$$

Remember that type size is the *height* of an entire typeface, essentially from the top of the highest character to the bottom of the lowest one.

Some typefaces, like Cochin, have really long ascenders and descenders:

long ascender ——

dpx } *little room for basic lower case letters*

long descender ——

As a result, there's not much height left for the basic lower case letters—and they get squeezed into a small vertical space. They look smaller and are harder to read in small point sizes.

On the other hand, some typefaces, like Avant Garde, have really short ascenders and descenders:

short ascender — dpx } *plenty of room for basic lower case letters*
short descender —

As a result, there's plenty of height left for the basic lower case letters—and the typeface is more readable at smaller sizes.

So now let's put this discussion of typefaces all together with some recommendations (there are samples of all these typefaces at the end of the chapter):

- *Times New Roman.* This serif typeface looks small on the page in 12-point type because the typeface is compressed. I prefer 13-point type but 12½ may suffice.

- *New Baskerville, New Century Schoolbook, and Palatino.* These serif typefaces look all right in 12-point type; however, I lean toward 12½ for New Baskerville and Palatino. They're a little more compressed than New Century Schoolbook.

- *Arial and Helvetica.* These sans serif typefaces make excellent headings. They both are not very compressed and have large lower case letters. As a result, they can be in bold type without the letters filling in. (You've probably seen letters like *o* and *d* and *p* in boldface with type filling into the middle.)

- *Avant Garde.* This is big—really big—for its point size. It's a very expanded sans serif typeface and has large lower case letters. As a result, Avant Garde works well in bold type, remaining readable in small sizes.

Be careful with full justification

Much of the time full justification is appropriate but not always. Here's the explanation.

There are three types of justification:

- *Full justification.* Both left and right margins are even.

- *Left justification.* Only the left margin is even; the right is ragged.

- *Right justification.* Only the right margin is even; the left is ragged.

Here is a sample of each:

Fully justified. This paragraph is fully justified. This paragraph is fully justified. This paragraph is fully justified. This paragraph is fully justified. This paragraph is fully justified. This paragraph is fully justified.

Left justified. This paragraph is left justified. This paragraph is left justified. This paragraph is left justified. This paragraph is left justified. This paragraph is left justified. This paragraph is left justified.

Right justified. This paragraph is right justified. This paragraph is right justified. This paragraph is right justified. This paragraph is right justified. This paragraph is right justified. This paragraph is right justified.

With most typefaces, either full justification or left justification is fine. Right justification is for special effects. The title on a cover page, for example, sometimes looks nice with right justification.

You want to avoid full justification with primarily one type-face: Courier. With Courier (and some of its relatives), full justification tends to leave uneven gaps between some of the words. I'm sure you've seen the problem. The uneven spacing makes the text harder to read.

The problem is that Courier is a monospaced typeface. Courier was an extremely popular choice of typewriter ball for the old IBM Selectric typewriter. Like most typewriter typefaces, each letter and number took up the *same width* on the page (hence, *mono*spaced):

ilmw

Notice that the normally narrow letters—*i* and *l*—are pretty wide. And the normally wide letters—*m* and *w*—are pretty narrow. Each character in Courier has the same width. As a result, there are few spacing tools for the printer to play with to make fully justified lines. If a big word won't quite fit at the end of the line, it moves to the next line. That leaves big spaces in the line above.

Tip

> *Avoid Courier unless you have a really good reason to use it. Courier looks like an old-fashioned typewriter did it. I've taken many straw polls, and clear majorities are tired of Courier.*

Proportional typefaces, on the other hand, have a much easier time with full justification. Here's a sample of a proportional typeface:

ilmw

Notice that the *i* and *l* are much narrower than the *m* and *w*. Because the characters have varying widths (and the space character can vary), proportional typefaces have more "tools" to stop the gaps.

So *avoid* full justification with Courier and any other monospaced typefaces you may have. But with proportional typefaces—Times New Roman, Palatino, and all the others we've talked about in this chapter—full justification and left justification both work well.

Restrict bold to titles and headings

Bold and *italics* both emphasize your words:

- Bold emphasizes a lot. It **stands out** from several feet away. That can be good or bad. It works great for headings. It can distract needlessly when you use it to emphasize words in paragraphs (as here).

- Italics emphasizes a little. It *stands out* when you're actually reading the words—not from several feet away.

I recommend that you use bold for your title and most of your headings and seldom anyplace else.

Use italics to emphasize text within paragraphs

If you've used bold for the major elements of your document, italics then works nicely for items of lesser emphasis—especially for words *within* paragraphs. Italics gives more emphasis than normal upright text but less emphasis than bold. It emphasizes when you need to without needlessly distracting your reader.

Sample typefaces

Here are samples of most of the typefaces we've talked about in the chapter. Look closely at how many words are on the first line of each sample. You'll see, for example, that Courier is really expanded and Times New Roman is really compressed. Also notice the overall look of the typeface and whether it appeals to you.

Times New Roman

This is a sample of 12-point type to help you compare typefaces. This is a sample of 12-point type to help you compare typefaces. This is a sample of 12-point type to help you compare typefaces.

Courier

This is a sample of 12-point type to help you compare typefaces. This is a sample of 12-point type to help you compare typefaces. This is a sample of 12-point type to help you compare typefaces

New Baskerville

This is a sample of 12-point type to help you compare typefaces. This is a sample of 12-point type to help you compare typefaces. This is a sample of 12-point type to help you compare typefaces.

(This is the typeface for the main text in this book.)

New Century Schoolbook

This is a sample of 12-point type to help you compare typefaces. This is a sample of 12-point type to help you compare typefaces. This is a sample of 12-point type to help you compare typefaces.

Palatino

This is a sample of 12-point type to help you compare typefaces. This is a sample of 12-point type to help you compare typefaces. This is a sample of 12-point type to help you compare typefaces.

Arial

This is a sample of 12-point type to help you compare typefaces. This is a sample of 12-point type to help you compare typefaces. This is a sample of 12-point type to help you compare typefaces.

Avant Garde

This is a sample of 12-point type to help you compare typefaces. This is a sample of 12-point type to help you compare typefaces. This is a sample of 12-point type to help you compare typefaces.

(This is the typeface for most headings in this book.)

Optima

This is a sample of 12-point type to help you compare typefaces. This is a sample of 12-point type to help you compare typefaces. This is a sample of 12-point type to help you compare typefaces.

Tip

Print a full page of one of your typical documents in several typefaces and sizes. Compare them. You'll probably have a clear preference right away.

❖   ❖   ❖

As you've seen, there are some important things to know about typefaces, but there are few rights and wrongs. Look at the wonderful ways professionals use type in books and magazines. Then start experimenting until you get the look you like.

CHAPTER 12

Headings

Bottom line

A good layout for headings can help your readers <u>see</u> the structure of your writing; a bad layout may only confuse them. Headings are a key that you can use in almost every document.

Good headings can make a terrific difference in most of your documents! At a glance, your reader can see that your documents *look* organized.

Headings also help show where the parts of your documents begin and end. Headings make nice reference points when your reader is trying to find something again. And they help you organize your thoughts in the first place.

But just having headings isn't good enough. Too often, people use confusing layouts for headings. This chapter will cover some fundamentals that will help your headings work for your readers.

Here's a summary of my tips for headings:

- Put more space above a heading than below it.
- Make sub-headings clearly subordinate to your main headings.
- Use at least two of each kind of heading.

At the end, I'll show you some sample headings.

Put more space above a heading than below it

A heading can do more than signal a new topic. It can also help group all the text for that topic.

The example on the left doesn't; the one on the right does:

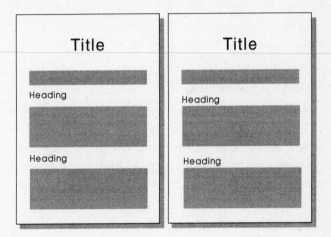

See the difference? The headings in the left sample float between sections; the headings on the right are clearly attached to something—the blocks of information that they label.

Make sub-headings clearly subordinate to your main headings

Headings label blocks of information. Sometimes you may have subdivided your blocks into parts and want to label them, too. So you need headings *and* sub-headings.

Here is an illustration:

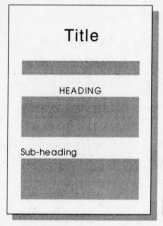

What you don't want to do, however, is to have headings that mislead your reader. Notice that the first heading looks subordinate to the next one, the sub-heading:

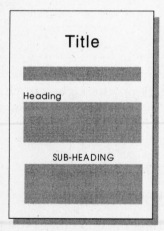
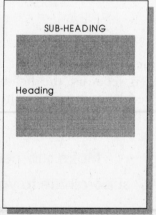

The sub-heading, which is upper case and centered, looks more important than the main heading, doesn't it? When you design your headings, you need to be sure they work with the priority your readers have learned—perhaps unconsciously—from having read thousands and thousands of pages of printed material. So when you choose the styles you want for your headings, you have to be careful to observe this hierarchy of importance:

- Upper case has priority over lower case:

THIS IS A HEADING / This is a heading

That is, if we see a heading that's all upper case, we'll probably figure that it labels a higher level section than a heading that's mainly lower case.

- Bold has priority over italics:

This is a heading / *This is a heading*

Again, we'll assume a bold heading probably labels a higher level section than a heading that's in italics. That's because bold tends to stand out more.

- Sans serif has priority over serif (if your main text is serif):

This is a heading / This is a heading

We'll probably assume that a sans serif heading labels a higher level section than a heading using the same serif typeface as the main text.

- A large type size has priority over a small type size:

This is a heading / This is a heading

Also:

- More space above and below a heading has priority over less.
- Centered has priority over starting on the left margin.
- A line from margin to margin underneath a heading gives priority over a heading without one.

Use at least two of each kind of heading

When readers see a heading, they automatically think—as a result of their experience—that they're seeing the first of several sections like that. In other words, they'd be surprised to find out that your document looks like this:

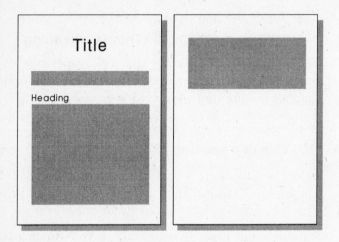

But this next one works with your reader's expectations:

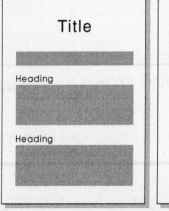

Sample headings

There is a nearly limitless number of ways to make headings. This section shows you just a few samples. In each case, notice that the sub-heading is subordinate to the main heading in at least *two* ways.

That is, if the main heading is upper case and centered, the sub-heading shouldn't be the same except that it starts on the left margin. The main heading and sub-heading would look too similar. When readers turn to a page with only one heading, they might not remember if it's your main heading or your sub-heading.

But if your sub-headings are different in at least two ways, your readers are more likely to immediately tell whether a single heading on a page is the main one or the subordinate one. For example, there are three differences between the main and sub-headings in this example. Can you spot them?

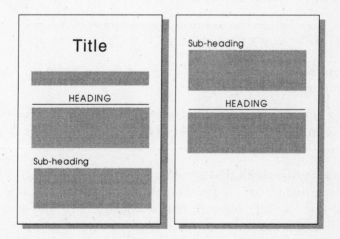

Here are the three differences—each giving priority to the main heading over the layout of the sub-heading:

- The main heading has a line under it from margin to margin.

- The main heading is centered.

- The main heading is all upper case.

Now let's look at another way to make headings:

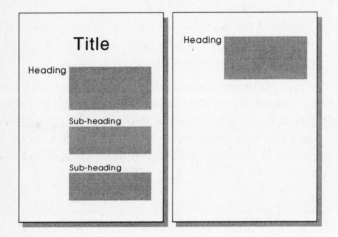

These main headings—the ones on the left margin—are "hanging headings."

They're quite common today for reports because of the white space they add. The page seems open and accessible, doesn't it?

Some people think that hanging headings waste space and make a document longer. Actually, though, the document gets only a little longer. That's because you can use a smaller type size for your main text.

Remember that the length of your line is important in choosing a type size. Because the hanging heading reduces the length of your line of main text, a smaller size works fine.

How much smaller? A point or so.

Tip

Use headings on most documents longer than about half a page. Even short documents benefit markedly from headings.

There can be a problem with hanging headings, though: you have to know how to work with two columns on your computer—one column for your headings, another for your text.

If you're not comfortable working with columns, a similar style of headings is easy to do:

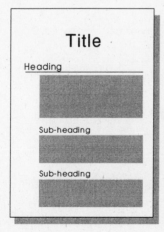 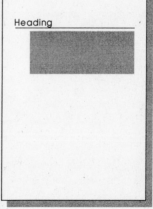

With this style, you simply indent your text more than you indent your main headings.

✜   ✜   ✜

There are many, many more ways to make headings. Look around, experiment, and find the ones that give the look you want for your document.

CHAPTER 13

Bullets

Bottom line

As with headings, a good layout for bullets can help your readers <u>*see*</u> *the structure of your writing; a bad layout may only confuse them.*

As you can tell, I consider the bullet a magical device, a wonderful way to help untangle ideas and show readers the organization within paragraphs.

In Chapter 4, we looked at bulleted *lists*. This chapter looks at bulleted *paragraphs* and then discusses ways to add polish to the way you present both bulleted lists and bulleted paragraphs.

Let's start with the bulleted paragraph.

What is a bulleted paragraph?

You needn't feel that bullets show only single sentences, like this:

> After 3 months of examining your records for the past year, we have found the following:
>
> - Your marketing division is systematically hiding its losses each month—totaling $300,000 for the past 6 months alone.

- The division manager and her assistant appear to be the only people involved.

- There were no other major discrepancies.

You can also have short paragraphs as bullets:

After 3 months of examining your records for the past year, we have found the following:

- Your marketing division is systematically hiding its losses each month—totaling $300,000 for the past 6 months alone. This may have been taking place for years—we did not have access to your records before last June.

- The division manager and her assistant appear to be the only people involved now. Some former employees may have been involved, however. For example, the former budget clerk just bought a Mercedes sports car and has moved to Hawaii. Perhaps he was involved, too.

Why use bulleted paragraphs? The usual answer: they show your reader the organization of your document. Notice that normal paragraphing doesn't do that:

After 3 months of examining your records for the past year, we have found the following:

Your marketing division is systematically hiding its losses each month—totaling $300,000 for the past 6 months alone. This may have been taking place for years—we did not have access to your records before last June.

The division manager and her assistant appear to be the only people involved now. Some former employees may have been involved, however. For example, the former budget clerk just bought a Mercedes sports car and has moved to Hawaii. Perhaps he was involved, too.

All three of those paragraphs look the same, as though they're at the same level of subordination. Actually, as we've seen, the second and third paragraphs are subordinate to the first. Bulleted paragraphs show that relationship better.

What symbol should you use for bullets?

There isn't just one symbol for bullets. Here are some perfectly acceptable ways for making the bullet symbol:

- • This is the traditional symbol.

- ■ This bullet is common, too. It echoes the rectangular shapes on many pages (paragraphs, illustrations, etc.). You may need to reduce its point size to make it look right.

- ♦ This bullet adds flair. Again, you may need to reduce its point size.

- – This is what people often use when they can't figure out how to get the other symbols out of their computers.

These ways all work fine, but you wouldn't want to use all of them in the same list, as I've done here.

By the way, if you check newspapers and magazines, you can find many different bullet symbols: squiggles, check marks, happy faces, graphic art (drawings of small pencils, for example), and so forth. These have their places, too, depending on the tone you want to set.

What spacing should you use for bulleted lists and paragraphs?

The reason for using bulleted lists and paragraphs is to isolate and group information, so you want to use plenty of white space. Here's a bulleted list that does just about everything wrong:

> After 3 months of examining your records for the past
> year, we have found the following:
> •Your marketing division is systematically hiding its
> losses each month—totaling $300,000 for the past 6
> months alone.
> •The division manager and her assistant appear be the
> only people involved.
> •There were no other major discrepancies.
> The attached report discusses these three findings.

Not effective, is it? I suggest double spacing between bulleted items (especially if any one of them is more than a line long). Here are some other tips on spacing:

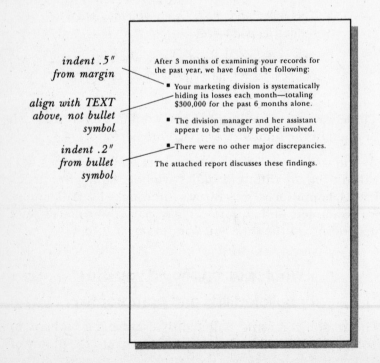

This spacing will help you "show off" your list so it can gain the attention it deserves.

How should you punctuate bulleted lists?

When you're using bulleted *paragraphs,* you don't have to worry about using special punctuation—just punctuate normally.

However, when you're using bulleted *lists,* you may wonder whether to start with a capital letter and whether to put a period at the end. After all, some lists are only words or phrases.

There are two common methods: the traditional method and the contemporary method (which I learned from Dr. Ginny Redish).

The traditional method—still quite popular—simply keeps the punctuation the list would have if it were part of a normal paragraph. Here's a list that's part of a normal paragraph—it's not bulleted yet:

> The order was late on April 15, late on April 16, and on time on April 17.

The traditional method would keep that same punctuation, pretending the list is still part of a regular sentence:

> The order was:
>
> - late on April 15,
>
> - late on April 16, and
>
> - on time on April 17.

The contemporary method—gaining popularity—stops the pretense that there's a sentence and gets rid of the commas, the period, and the word *and*:

The order was:

- late on April 15

- late on April 16

- on time on April 17

Where's the period to end the sentence? I don't know. There simply isn't one. But readers are more likely to notice a period *there* than a period *missing*. The contemporary method places more importance on each item in the list having the same appearance than on pretending the list is still a "sentence."

So here's how the contemporary method handles punctuation and capitalization:

- If the bulleted item is a sentence, make it look like one (that is, start with a capital letter and put a period at the end).

- If the bulleted item is *not* a sentence, don't. That is, don't start with a capital letter and don't put any punctuation at the end.

Let's look at several examples. You've seen the next one before. Notice that the items in it are not sentences, so they don't begin with capital letters or end with periods:

The order was:

- late on April 15

- late on April 16

- on time on April 17

Now let's rewrite that example to make the items into sentences. Notice that they now look like sentences—with capital letters and periods:

Here's what happened to the orders:

- They were late on April 15.

- They were late on April 16.

- They were on time on April 17.

Tip _____

Be sure your lists are parallel. That is, lists should never have some items that are full sentences and some that aren't. Once you set up a pattern for a list, you must stick to it—<u>*all*</u>* full sentences or* <u>*all*</u> *only phrases.*

_____

Sometimes you have items that are only phrases but then you want to add a comment or two. What do you do? Well, here's a solution involving a little rewriting:

Here's what happened:

- *April 15.* The order was 15 minutes late (arriving at 9:15).

- *April 16.* The order was 35 minutes late (arriving at 9:35).

- *April 17.* The order was on time (arriving at 8:55).

This combines the topics of the last two chapters—bullets *and* headings. They work well separately; they work well together. And both make the reader's job much easier.

✣   ✣   ✣

Now for the final chapter on layout: graphics.

CHAPTER 14

Graphics

Bottom line

Today's writers need to get beyond paragraphs full of words. Tables, drawings, graphs, and other illustrations are often what readers remember most.

If you look at a page with an illustration on it, don't you look at the illustration first? And if you look at a page with nothing but paragraphs full of words, don't you wish there were an illustration there?

I imagine most of us have learned to value illustrations. There are some obvious types of illustrations. For example:

- If you want to show how your profits have increased over the past five years, use a line graph or bar chart.

- If you're talking about the gill structure of an obscure tropical fish, use a drawing.

- If you want to show the latest Parisian design for an evening gown, show a photograph.

Those are all useful. They'll have impact. And your readers will remember them.

These types of graphics are all good, but you already know about them. This chapter talks about some other techniques. Whenever you find yourself struggling to describe something in paragraphs full of words, maybe one of these can help:

- using a creative layout for your words
- using a highlighted figure
- including the object itself
- using a diagram

Using a creative layout for your words

Sometimes you can creatively place your words on the page. The effect is to draw your reader to that information.

For example, a simple table can clearly show your logic. Here's one showing options for producing a large, complex report:

Option	Advantages	Disadvantages
Do it manually.	No computer costs.	Takes forever.
Give everybody a big, powerful, expensive computer to process the data.	People get reports more quickly.	High cost of computers.
Give everybody a less powerful, cheaper computer AND one big, powerful, expensive computer for the entire group.	People get reports more quickly AND costs are cheaper.	None.

This logic table makes the writer's point much more quickly than the same ideas in a few paragraphs.

Here's another example of a creative way to present words. In this case, a woman is describing her position as a "floater" in a law office's secretarial pool:

F flexibility. This is the key to being effective. I sit at a secretary's station surrounded by *that* person's equipment and *that* person's organization of files. My job is to familiarize myself with these as quickly as possible.

L legal secretarial skills. I must be able to type quickly (at least 80 wpm), take shorthand, and use the computer network efficiently.

O other duties as assigned. I have performed such duties as notarizing documents, inventorying supplies, boxing files for storage, and logging in billing information.

A ability to work every machine. I must be able to use the many different computers as well as more than one kind of copier, fax machine, transcriber, etc.

T telephone savvy. For those attorneys who do not answer their telephone lines, I have to know when it is appropriate to interrupt to announce an incoming call.

E editing skills. Much of my work involves correcting an attorney's product.

R receptionist skills. On rare occasions, I sit in for one of our four receptionists. I dislike this job the most. If I hear they are looking for someone to cover the phones, I hide out in the bathroom!

Using a highlighted example

The highlighted example is another way to present words in a more visual way. Here's the illustration that accompanied a description of "National Stock Number":

Digits 1 - 4:
Federal Stock Class

Digits 5 - 13:
National Item Identification Number

1006 - 00 - 123 - 4567

country code   serial number

The writer then explained each part of the number and gave an example. The labels at the bottom—"country code" and "serial number"—are "callouts." They point to information on an illustration and are extremely useful.

Including the object itself

I once read a memo discussing fiber optics. The author taped a sample on the first page. Believe me, one strand took up little space. Perhaps there are times you're describing something that is small and cheap enough to attach.

Using a diagram

A diagram is a good way to describe something with several components. In this, the writer showed the hidden costs that businesses recover in order to be profitable:

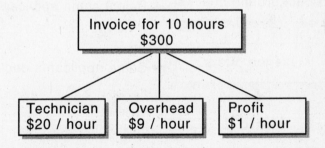

Tip

Once you write a longer document, consciously look it over for places to add graphics (or to replace paragraphs with graphics).

And here's another one showing the hiring process for a large organization (as you review it, imagine trying to say the same thing in paragraphs full of words):

⁂   ⁂   ⁂

Images like these take a little creativity, but they make a world of difference for your readers.

FINAL WORDS

CHAPTER 15

The writing process

Bottom line

A good writing process makes getting words on the page easier.

So far this book has been totally concerned with the *product* of your writing: your document should have a clear style, start with the bottom line, and use good layout.

This chapter is about the *process* of writing. It shows how you can get words on paper easily.

What's a good writing process?

Is this the writing process you learned?

Prewriting
1. Think hard.
2. Write an outline.

Writing
1. Follow your outline.
2. Write quickly without worrying about revisions.

Rewriting
1. Make sure you followed your outline.
2. Fix any errors.

Well, there's surely some truth there, but there are some half-truths, too.

The role of the outline

What's the role of an outline? Should you have one? Most business people I speak with confess: they rarely use an outline, and they virtually never use a formal outline (you know—I, A, B, II, A, B).

Outlines do have advantages, though. It's always helpful to know where you're going before you start. But sometimes writers simply aren't quite sure where they're going *until* they write; that is, as they struggle to put thoughts into those elusive things called words, learning takes place: new ideas emerge and old ideas take new shape. We've all had that experience.

In other words, sometimes we have trouble writing an effective outline at the beginning of the writing process. Starting "cold" seems to produce either bad outlines or, worse, only a blank piece of paper and a deep sense of guilt.

For something under a page or so, don't worry about an outline at all. It probably isn't necessary. For something longer—even just slightly longer—an outline may be helpful. Here's what I recommend:

- If you have excellent understanding of your content at the start, try making an outline. Don't worry about those Roman numerals—just jot something down. You may want to jot down only main headings.

- If you're a little unsure of your content, try jotting down several ideas in the order you think you should cover them. Then start writing. After writing two or three paragraphs, you'll probably warm up; that is, your mind will be focused on your material—more saturated with the information you want to cover. So reassess your outline and redo it if necessary—this time perhaps in a little more detail.

- If you're embarking on a long writing project or one involving other writers, work hard to get a good—even formal—outline on paper before you begin.

A "recursive" process

Researchers today believe that most writing doesn't take place in a linear order: first prewriting, then writing, then rewriting. Rather, there's lots of moving back and forth. Researchers call that "recursiveness."

But . . . a linear draft

Even though your writing process may be recursive, your draft should usually be linear. That is, you should start at the beginning and work your way straight through. The other way—writing part 2 before part 1, for example—can cause problems.

Here's why. If you have a good organization, your reader will read the document in order: page 1, then page 2, then page 3. So for you to write page 3, you need to know what the reader has already seen on pages 1 and 2. It's amazing how often good writing refers to earlier material—or depends on it.

The final version of a good document is like a tapestry—all threads are important to the final design, and all threads are in the right place.

My own writing process

What happens on a typical writing project—something two or three pages long? Or even book length? What would be a good way to write that document?

We all have our special techniques, but here's what normally happens when I write:

1. I fool myself into believing I'm actually ready to write, so I start in.

2. I get stuck.

3. I then jot down a quick list of the main points I want to cover. If I can think of any subpoints, I put them in, too.

4. I arrange those points in the best order.

5. I start writing again.

6. If I find that I'm not following my original outline, I don't worry: my ideas while I'm actually writing are probably much better than my ideas beforehand.

7. I rarely get stuck again, but if I do, I re-outline (briefly).

8. I write quickly, with no thought for typos or other errors.

9. But I stop *immediately* if the content or organization isn't working. After all, what comes before is crucial to what comes after, so I must get the content and organization right. Otherwise, I'm wasting my time because I know I'll have to rewrite significantly.

10. When I finish writing, I read and revise immediately.

11. I then set the writing aside for awhile—even a few minutes helps disconnect my mind from the particular words on the paper.

12. Then I reread and revise, looking not just for errors but for the important matters this book covers (style, organization, and layout). Throughout, I ask these questions: "Will my reader understand?" and "Have I made my points the best way possible?"

13. Then I show the writing to someone else for feedback. I try to "lean toward" their suggestions rather than away from them. But I realize that I am the one

most responsible for the content *and* the most engaged with it, so I take "my" advice before theirs.

14.   I watch reruns of *Cheers* on television.

Frankly, I follow that process much of the time I write. It works for me.

Normally I write about 5 pages or so at a sitting. Later I'll read and revise those pages before starting a new section. That way I'm familiar with what I've just written before starting the writing again; also, I'll have fairly polished pages as I move along.

What if there's not enough time?

You may not always have time to do all that. Well, the more comfortable you are with plain English, the faster and better you will be able to write.

Still, sometimes you can't put your writing aside. True. And sometimes you can't show your writing to someone else. True. But lots of times you *can*—and *should*.

Tip

Especially for those "career" projects that come up once or twice a year, build in the opportunity for the two feedback steps—feedback from someone else and feedback from yourself (after getting away from the writing for awhile).

CHAPTER 16

Supervising writers

Bottom line

Your people depend on __you__ for guidance on how to write.

I know that not everybody who reads this book is a supervisor (or project leader). Some people are and many hope to be. So if you are now, this chapter is for you. And if you're not one yet? Well, this chapter is what I would tell your boss.

So . . . for supervisors—present and future: do you ever get frustrated by the writing your people do? If so, you're among the vast majority of supervisors.

Some people just don't understand the English language very well; most people, however, write "that way"—bureaucratically—because they believe they have to. They think that's the kind of writing *you want:* stilted, overly formal, passive, and "impressive."

After all, if you ever wrote in the bureaucratic style, didn't you write that way because you felt "that's what the boss wants"?

So what can you do to improve the writing of your people, to help them understand—and apply—the principles of plain English?

Here are a few tips:

Get good word processing

Make sure your people aren't still in the dark ages—get software that's up to date. Word processing from a previous generation just isn't capable of producing top-notch, professional documents.

Tell your people what you want

Remember in school when you got a paper back with red marks all over it and a comment like this: "Sentences must never begin with *and* or *but*. Don't start sentences that way in my class!" Don't you wish the teacher had told you that *before* you handed in the paper?

The same thing happens when your people write for you— if you haven't told them what you want. In fact, I suggest you tell your people in a memo that you want plain English. Tell them to write the way they talk, use pronouns, use headings, use contractions—everything. And let your memo illustrate those techniques. Then people will see the new style in action—with your signature on it.

You can use the memo time and again as you move on to new positions or as new people come to work for you. In fact, I've worked with organizations where the president's memo on writing was one of the first pieces of paper a new employee received.

Show them examples of good writing

While examples of bad writing are all over the place, examples of good writing are sometimes hard to find. But when you have such an example, you have gold. People can do an amazing job following a good example: "Oh, *that's* what you want!"

When a good example *does* cross your desk, by all means send it to all your writers—and then congratulate the person who wrote it.

When a good example does *not* ever cross your desk, then you need to take a harder step. You need to create a good example. You can do that two ways:

- You can write the example yourself.

- You can get a good writer to write one for you.

The effort, believe me, is worth it. And if you can't find a good example from your people's writing, the effort is *especially* necessary—and *especially* worth it.

Tell them when they write well for you—or badly

I know: you don't have time to give feedback to your writers. One reason you don't have time may be that you're dealing with too much of their bad writing. They'll keep turning it out, though, unless you intervene. Make an effort at least once to give detailed feedback to each writer.

Don't forget to tell them what they're doing right. If you don't give them reinforcement, they may never know what you like and may well change to something worse.

In summary . . .

Good writing is worth the effort, from you and from your people.

The simple writing techniques in this book—on style, organization, and layout—can make all the difference to writers, readers, supervisors.

So push for plain English—it's the new way to write!

APPENDIX

Simpler words and phrases

Bureaucratic	Better
accompany	go with
accomplish	do
advise	tell, recommend
afford an opportunity	let
anticipate	expect
approximately	about
ascertain	find out
assist	help
at the present time	now
attached herewith is	here's
benefit	help
close proximity	near
commence	begin
complete	fill out
conclude	end
concur	agree
cooperate	help
deem	think
demonstrate	show, prove
desire	want
determine	find out
disclose	show
effect	make
elect	choose
endeavor	try

Bureaucratic	**Better**
ensue	follow
exhibit	show
experience	have
facilitate	help
failed to	didn't
forward	send
furnish	send
furthermore	also
has the capability	can
however	but
identical	same
implement	carry out, do
in addition	also
in an effort to	to
in lieu of	instead of
in the event that	if
in the near future	soon
inasmuch as	since
inception	start
incumbent upon	must
indicate	show
initial	first
initiate	start
insufficient	not enough
legislation	law
limited number	few
locate	find
location	place
maintain	keep, support
modify	change
monitor	check, watch
notify	let someone know
numerous	many, most
observe	see

Bureaucratic   Better

Bureaucratic	Better
permit	let
personnel	people
presently	now
prior to	before
provided that	if
purchase	buy
relating to	about, on
request	ask
require	need
residence	home
retain	keep
reveal	show
review	check, go over
state	say
submit	send
subsequent	later, next
sufficient	enough
supply	send
terminate	stop
therefore	so
this office	we, us
time period	time
transmit	send
transpire	happen
until such time as	until
utilization	use
utilize	use
viable	workable
whereas	since
witnessed	saw

Index